D1811091

How to pass examinations in
Personnel Management

K. J. Pratt, M.Sc., F.C.I.S., A.I.P.M.
Head of School of Administrative Studies,
Chelmer Essex Institute of Higher Education,

and

S. G. Bennett, A.C.I.S., M.Inst.M., M.Inst.A.M.(Dip).
Principal Lecturer in Administrative Studies,
Chelmer Essex Institute of Higher Education

Cassell • London

CASSELL LTD.
Greycoat House, 10 Greycoat Place, London SW1P 1SB

an affiliate of Macmillan Publishing Co. Inc.,
New York

First published 1982

ISBN 0 304 30961 3

Set in 10/11 pt English Times Compugraphic
by Colset Pte Ltd, Singapore

Printed and bound in Great Britain at
The Camelot Press Ltd, Southampton

For whom is this book intended?

This book is specifically recommended to students of the following professional bodies:

The Association of Certified Accountants
The Chartered Building Societies Institute
The Institute of Administrative Management
The Institute of Bankers
The Institute of Chartered Secretaries and Administrators
The Institute of Personnel Management

sitting both personnel management and other management papers. The coverage of subjects relevant to these papers is amply demonstrated by the range of questions in this book.

Similar questions will also be encountered by those studying for a variety of qualifications in these areas, eg

BEC Higher National Certificate and Diploma
Diploma and Certificate in Management Studies
Various degree courses
Other professional bodies

Contents

1 Approaching examinations in personnel management and related subjects

In writing this book we have attempted to utilise our experience as examinees as well as lecturers and examiners. We try to take a view from both sides of the fence and look at all aspects of the activity known as 'exams' to provide what we hope will be useful guidance.

The sections which follow are an attempt to break down the subject into identifiable areas. When dealing with examination questions it is often difficult to categorise them and, of necessity, their inclusion in one section or another is sometimes arbitrary and often subjective. Despite this difficulty we hope that this system will help you with your revision particularly when up against 'problem topics'.

All of the sections follow a similar format:

Introduction – A brief discussion of the subject area, the type of knowledge and skills required and the types of examination question to be expected.

Sample examination question(s) – An actual question taken from a recent paper of one of the professional bodies which examine in the subject.

Key points – An outline of what we consider to be some of the essential features of a sound answer to the question.

Suggested answer – A form of answer which covers the points which we consider important and which should be attainable within the usual 30–40 minutes allocated by most examinations.

Further examination questions – A cross-section of typical examination questions taken from recent papers of various professional bodies.

General comments on questions – Each of the selected questions is discussed, looking both at technical content and what we think the examiner is looking for in approach and treatment.

Recommended reading – A brief selection of reading relevant to each section which we consider to be useful for those who feel a need for further study in a particular area.

Examination questions

All examination questions in this book are used with permission and are taken from recent papers of the following bodies:

Association of Certified Accountants (ACA)
Chartered Building Societies Institute (CBSI)
Institute of Administrative Management (IAM)
Institute of Bankers (IOB)
Institute of Chartered Secretaries and Administrators (ICSA)
Institute of Personnel Management (IPM)

We should like to thank these bodies for allowing us to use their past questions but must make it clear, of course, that none of our comments and suggestions have been officially approved or have any connection with the bodies concerned.

Although the particular source of all the examination questions used is identified, it is worth mentioning that similarly worded questions are often found in the papers of other professional bodies. It is not practical to include all the minor variations, but you should not disregard a question just because it does not come from your own particular professional body. We have endeavoured to select a representative cross-section of the questions on the topic concerned.

Examination questions tend to fall into two main categories – the direct 'subject-based' question and the more general question which might embrace several areas of knowledge. As mentioned earlier, we found it difficult in some cases to allocate a question to a particular section. Part of the skill of dealing with questions is, of course, the initial interpretation and identification of the particular areas of skill and knowledge which the examiner is attempting to test. Although some questions deliberately provide an opportunity for a wide-ranging answer, we fear that others are unintentionally ambiguous due to poor drafting. In the latter situation we can only suggest that you either choose an alternative question or state clearly on the paper any assumptions which you make concerning the basic meaning of the question.

Examiners

Behind every examination paper there is an examiner. Although candidates often think of them as faceless automatons, they are, of course, human – or almost! Many candidates, in our experience, tend to forget this and it can be to their disadvantage.

Personnel management and its related disciplines provide an opportunity for a fair amount of subjectivity, not to mention bias. Although examiners should be as objective as humanly possible, they do have their personal quirks and pre-judices. Careful study of past examination papers and (more important) examiners' reports can often be most revealing. Many examiners have strong views, not only upon the subject-matter of the questions but on such things as style and layout.

We like to think that personnel management examiners in particular are sufficiently flexible and broad-minded to accept that there is often no such thing as a 'model answer' and that each script should be marked on its merits. Having said this, however, we feel that it does no harm from the candidate's point of view to 'get to know' his examiner and, dare we say, patronise him a little. If, for instance, it is clear from previous examiners' reports that he likes to see reference to practical examples and illustrations, it seems only sensible to try to supply them.

The examination

Examinations in personnel management and related subjects require much of the preparation and technique considered prudent for most exams. But in common with most subjects, personnel management contains certain idiosyncrasies which need to be recognised and given attention.

Many books have been written about examination technique and we do not intend to go into the sort of detail which many of these provide. However, we feel that it is appropriate to pass on what amounts to a distillation of a wide range of knowledge, advice, and recommendation from a variety of sources, including our own bitter experience.

Prior to the examination

In our experience, students often consider that personnel management is a 'waffle' subject requiring little expertise and consequently little preparation. A short time spent reading examiners' reports would both verify the existence of this attitude and show how sadly wrong it is. The cliché that 'there is no substitute for hard work' applies equally to personnel management as to other subjects. So what should you do to be properly prepared for the examination? Apart from a suitable course of study, the following checklist gives what we consider to be the minimum actions required by someone who is anticipating an examination in Personnel Management and related subjects.

1 Read the syllabus – this may or may not be helpful but cannot be ignored (see **2** below).

2 Study past examination papers – these are usually a better indicator of what to expect than the syllabus. A pattern may be perceived if you obtain several papers – money well-spent.

3 Read a selection of examiners' reports (see 'Examiners' above).

4 Read recommended basic texts (at least one), including the first and last chapters! Wherever possible get hold of some of the supplementary texts to add breadth to your knowledge.

5 Keep abreast of current affairs by reference to relevant journals and quality newspapers.

6 Obtain copies of booklets and guides from the Department of Employment, ACAS etc. They are usually written in layman's language, often in note form and sometimes they are free.

7 Attempt skeleton answers to past exam questions and check to see if you have covered all the points.

8 Test yourself under examination conditions to get the 'feel' of the paper which you will be sitting.

During the examination

A well prepared candidate can still make fundamental errors under the stress of examination conditions. Again, we shall not go into great detail as there are many books on examination technique but we should like to draw your attention to some of the points which our experience has shown to be crucial.

1 Read the question. Then read it again! Consider the *whole* question and don't hook onto one word out of context. (See **2** below.)

2 Answer the question as set and not one which you would like to have been set. To quote a recent examiner's report, 'It is necessary to answer the question asked, and not some other question which only exists in the imagination of the candidate.' You will probably gain few marks for much effort and may have been better occupied answering another question.

3 Where questions contain two or more parts, whether specified or implied, make sure that you cover all parts and give them an appropriate weighting.

4 Allow time for thinking before tackling a question. In our experience some students consider that any time not spent writing is wasted, but 'quality rather than quantity' is a fairer guide.

5 A rough outline (in pencil) prior to starting the answer proper often helps to gather your thoughts and arrange the points into some logical sequence rather than plunging in and producing a disjointed answer. (Underline before starting answer and cross out neatly before proceeding to next question).

6 Look for 'clues' in the wording of the question which often provide guidance. Words and phrases such as *discuss*; *briefly discuss*; *draft in some detail*; *illustrate your answer*; *outline*; *write a report*, etc. should indicate the style of answer expected by the examiner.

7 Where questions call for 'advantages and disadvantages,' remember that there are various points of view. What is an 'advantage' to one party may be a 'disadvantage' to another.

8 Use examples drawn from your experience or reading where applicable as they often help to illustrate, reinforce and add interest to an answer.

9 Commit to memory legal and research references. You will be expected to support many statements with actual evidence and there can be little or no credit for errors. Spelling errors also tend to annoy some examiners.

10 Despite the controversial nature of many topics, don't allow your personal or political views to distort or replace a well balanced answer.

11 Finally, answer the number of questions requested and allocate time accordingly. Yes, it still happens, even if never to you, that candidates lose marks by failing to leave enough time for later questions.

Recommended reading

Pitfield, M. and Donnelly, R., *How to Take Examinations*, IPM, 1980.

2 The personnel function and the role of the personnel manager

Introduction

It is probable that as a result of your studies so far you have a fairly clear idea of the typical areas of responsibility of a modern personnel manager. These include:

Manpower planning – the determination of future staff requirements.

Employment – recruitment, interviewing, testing, transfers, promotions, dismissals, redundancy.

Labour relations – negotiations and administration of terms and conditions of employment, the maintenance of formal and informal channels of communication, grievance procedures.

Wage and salary administration – job analysis, job evaluation, incentive schemes, fringe benefits.

Education and training – induction, skills training, supervisor and management development, career development, organisation development.

Health and safety – industrial hygiene, safety enforcement, medical and first aid service provision.

Welfare – counselling facilities, staff discount schemes, canteen facilities, sports and social clubs, benevolent funds.

The personnel specialist's degree of involvement in these areas will naturally vary widely. In many instances his role will be purely advisory, while in others he will act in tandem with line managers. In very few situations is it likely that he will have the authority to act with total independence: indeed, in very few situations will it be practicable.

As a general perspective of the field the above description is satisfactory. In one sense, however, it is misleading, in as much as it suggests the existence of a commonly acknowledged entity known as 'personnel management'. This is far from the truth. Both amongst practitioners and academics there exists considerable disagreement about the precise role, responsibilities and indeed existence of such a specialism. The nature of the authority exercised by the function is commonly the subject of very real practical difficulty: this is discussed below. Other arguments have to do with the often apparent conflict between the personnel specialist's concern for people and his responsibilities as a manager. Some argue that, as a cohesive entity, personnel management simply does not exist; instead, that it comprises a collection of disparate activities discarded by others, or that it is merely a restatement of the skills and knowledge required by any manager irrespective of specialism: that *all* managers must by definition be personnel managers.

Sample examination question

'Staff and line conflicts are endemic in organisations, and call into question the utility of this form of structure.' Discuss this proposition with particular reference to the position of the personnel department.   *(ICSA)*

Key points

1 An explanation of the terms 'line' and 'staff'.

2 The practical problems of such a structure: the mutually emotive perception of rules and status by both line and staff managers.

3 The line manager's perception of the staff specialist.

4 The specialist's perception of the line manager.

5 The particular problems affecting the acceptability of the personnel function. The effects of legislation; the contradiction between adviser and policeman; interference in the manager/employee relationship; the existence or otherwise of an accepted personnel specialism.

6 Despite its intrinsic problems, the structure is empirically useful. The problems may be overcome. Resolution of the conflict; senior management's role; the specialist's role.

Suggested answer

Before considering the nature of the line-staff conflict it is worthwhile clarifying what is meant by the two terms 'line' and 'staff'. Managers occupying 'line' positions normally have executive authority and responsibility for all that occurs within their particular department or area of responsibility. Persons occupying 'staff' positions normally act as *advisers* to line management. Typically, production and sales are considered line functions, while personnel management together with other services such as public relations or data processing are considered staff.

For the line manager, the introduction of a staff specialist will often be perceived as a direct threat to his own status. Acceptance of the specialist and his advice may be considered a diminution of the line manager's authority. At the same time, refusal to accept advice may result in the matter being referred to senior management with the risk that it may subsequently be imposed, with yet more damaging effects on the status of the line manager concerned. The result is something of a 'Catch 22' situation, understandably resulting in frustration.

The imposition of the specialism will often be considered a demonstration by senior management that previous performance has been in some way inadequate. Alternatively it may be considered yet another obstacle thrown in the line manager's path, further frustrating his achievement of targets by the introduction of 'irrelevancies'.

Frequently the specialist will be head office based, the creation of the new specialism the brain-child of a member of senior management. Prudence will require therefore that he be treated with greater care than otherwise justified by his rank, still further hindering the development of a working relationship. Characteristically, the specialist will often be younger, better educated, and having attitudes, values and background very different to those of the line manager, his comparative youth prompting doubts regarding the basis of his advice. Like most specialists, he will inevitably have developed a professional jargon or shorthand. Intended to speed communication, this will often place yet further distance between him and the other man.

Equally the staff specialist may feel frustrated by his lack of authority to implement what he knows to be the best course of action. Such frustration will be heightened when advice is rejected on what are suspected to be emotive rather than objective grounds. Already irritated by the line manager's obvious antipathy, the specialist may himself find difficulty in concealing doubts regarding the other man's competence. Indeed, his response may very well be to ignore totally his advisory capacity, attempting instead to impose his will. In instances where his advice is sought, it is often only to discover that a once soluble problem has now adopted an irreversible trend. Such is the nature of the line-staff conflict.

So far as the personnel function is concerned, the situation is potentially still more complicated. Of the factors which have led to the rising importance of the specialism, one of the most influential is undoubtedly the effect of employment legislation which now encompasses most aspects of the employer-employee relationship, with often severe penalties for non-compliance. This has imposed two fundamental responsibilities on the personnel specialist: the translation of legislation into corporate policy, and the monitoring of line management activity, to ensure adherence. Such are radical modifications of the specialism's previous advisory role. From time to time, resulting policy may not be consistent with other corporate objectives. Thus, for example, adherence to safety regulations may well conflict with output targets. There is also an inherent contradiction in the role of adviser and policeman. Douglas McGregor indeed suggests that the two are incompatible. In exercising a monitoring role, the personnel manager penetrates to an increasing degree the relationship between manager and staff, such an intrusion providing wholly reasonable grounds for resentment.

A further problem has to do with the acceptability and to some degree the existence of personnel management as a specialism. Evidence shows clearly that certain specialisms are more acceptable than others. Such acceptability is determined by a number of factors, one of which is the existence or otherwise of a mutually accepted discipline. With its emphasis on the behavioural sciences, it is hardly surprising that much modern personnel theory and practice is treated with suspicion by those more used to the certainty of numeracy and the physical sciences. Indeed, many such managers would argue that as a specialism, personnel management simply does not exist – the skills and knowledge required being extensions of those needed by any manager.

Despite such problems, the continuing use of line and staff structures suggests that while problems exist, they are not insuperable. To a considerable degree the contribution of senior management will have much to do with creating an environment in which co-operation is likely to occur. The attitude of senior managers will invariably affect that of their subordinates, indications that a specialism is considered of importance to senior management providing the lead for those at lower levels. Such an indication may well be the appointment of a specialist to a senior management post, though clearly there are practical limitations to this. Situations may be created in which line management and specialists are brought together and required to commit their combined talents to the solution of a problem, in this way being exposed to each other's problems and potential contribution. An alternative technique intended to achieve similar results is staff rotation. A periodic emphasis of the *advisory* nature of staff specialists may also prove mutually valuable. Consideration may be given to decentralisation of the specialist function – advice given by a member of a local management team being often more acceptable than that handed down from a remote head office department.

So far as the staff specialist is concerned, it is probably realistic to say that his own attitude will to a considerable degree determine his prospects of success. The emphasis should be always on establishing a client-professional adviser relationship. Selection of initial tasks is an important consideration. Ideally, a problem should be selected that is known to be worrying the line manager, where demonstrable success is more likely than failure and which results in no adverse consequences for other groups.

Further examination questions

1 What practical problems are likely to face an employee who occupies a 'staff' as opposed to a 'line' role in an organisation?
(*ACA*)

2 Is the 'line and staff' relationship more complicated in the case of a personnel function than in the cases of other 'staff' functions? If so, in what ways? (*ICSA*)

3 What is the nature of the authority exercised by a personnel function? (*IPM*)

4 'Personnel policies and the techniques of personnel management all imply "something being done" by an organisation to or for its employees. But, if the personnel specialist is to carry out a creative role, it must be part of his day-to-day working philosophy to have regard for those employees as individual human beings.'
     Does this statement in any way contradict the personnel manager's role in management? (*CBSI*)

5 'Personnel specialists insist that they are there to help management

achieve its business goals; yet in their everyday activities they show themselves to be remote from those goals.' Is this a fair criticism?

(IPM)

6 In what ways can computers assist personnel departments to more effective fulfilment of their main functions? *(ICSA)*

General comments on questions

Questions 1 and 2 are essentially similar to the sample examination question, though in Question 1, the examiner does not specify that particular attention should be given to personnel activity.

Question 3 requires a development of the nature of the authority exercised by a personnel function. As outlined in the suggested answer, formal authority does not normally exist: the function occupies an advisory role. This must, however, be qualified in a number of ways:

a The consequences of legislation are to impose on the function an executive policy formulation and control role.

b The increasing tendency to appoint personnel specialists to senior management posts can only enhance its real rather than nominal authority.

c In practice, the reaction of many managers, after a period of initial resistance, is to willingly transfer personnel matters to a specialist in order that they may concentrate on more 'essential' matters.

d The consequences of change are to subject both organisation and individual workers to pressure, often resulting in unpredictable reactions. As the organisation's 'people expert', the personnel specialist has a role to play. Nominally, it is again advisory – but in practice the function's situational authority again imposes a policy-formulation role: in this instance, how to deal with change so as to minimise its negative consequences.

Questions 4 and 5 have to do with what one writer has described as the personnel function's 'identity crisis', a crisis summed up in an IPM statement published in 1963: 'Personnel management aims to achieve both efficiency and justice . . .'.

An examination of the development of the specialism reveals that its origins are to be found in middle-class, often religiously based, reaction to the squalid working conditions commonly found in the late eighteenth and early nineteenth centuries. As a result it has often been stamped with something of a moralistic, 'Lady Bountiful' image.

By many the personnel manager is seen as a 'man in the middle', a 'keeper of the corporate conscience' balancing the needs of workers against those of the organisation. To a degree, the image has been reinforced by the function's propensity to attract apparently unconnected responsibilities of a marginally welfare kind – the so-called 'trash-can hypothesis' — and by its preoccupation with the behavioural sciences. Though increasingly geared to the improvement of corporate effectiveness, this preoccupation has still further marked the personnel specialist as' seeking to hinder the achievement of organisational goals, promoting instead the interests of the workforce.

What such an attitude fails to recognise is that the development of the modern personnel function is an amalgam of two qualitatively distinct themes. That an underlying concern for welfare and justice exists is undeniable, but superimposed is the subsequently evolving, and greater, concern for effective labour management. Increases in trade union power, more recently reinforced by legislation, have changed radically the nature of the effective personnel manager's task. To some degree it has rendered untenable many of the earlier quasi-paternalistic attitudes. As discussed above (Question 3), change imposes further demands on the personnel specialist, bringing him into the very forefront of the fight for corporate survival.

To succeed, an organisation must manage its labour force as effectively as any other resource. The functions of the modern personnel manager are thus no different from those of any other manager. In classical terms, his functions are to plan, organise, motivate and control. In order that corporate objectives may be achieved, personnel plans, policies and procedures must be formulated. Staff must be organised, trained and equipped to carry out their tasks and motivated towards the willing achievement of determined goals. Such plans formulated and implemented, the remaining responsibility is to develop means of monitoring performance. In this way the activities of the personnel manager coincide precisely with those of both other managers and the organisation.

Question 6. Before the advent of electronic data processing (EDP), personnel records were kept in manual form in many organisations. While this proved wholly adequate for many purposes, it nevertheless limited, in most instances, the potential utility of the recorded data. The widespread availability of EDP, accelerated by budget-priced microprocessors, is prompting more and more organisations to realise that by storing employee details in computerised form, a significant contribution may be made to personnel decision-making, while at the same time releasing personnel staff from clerical drudgery to take a more active management role.

While the computer has a role to play in storing and reproducing records, such use scarcely scratches the surface of its greater capability. With greater attention focussed on integrated data processing systems, in most aspects of personnel management activity computer assistance is now available. Examples are:

1 *Manpower planning* – considerable use may be made of the computer's ability to develop mathematical models. Manipulating data of incredible complexity and despite the frequent absence of certainty, it is nevertheless possible, perhaps for the first time, to achieve a realistic basis for the development of manpower plans.

2 *Selection* – while the face-to-face interview seems unlikely ever to be wholly usurped, despite its limitations, some use has been made of EDP by organisations such as IBM for purposes of planning and monitoring selection procedures. Some use has also been made of computer systems as tools of selection testing and as means of improving objectivity in the interpretation of test results.

3 *Appraisal* – though little direct use of EDP appears to have occurred, it is apparent that a number of organisations, eg Texas Instruments, are using it as a means of improving the validity and reliability of appraisal procedures by mathematically comparing appraisal ratings with each other and with other objective criteria.

4 *Training* – available evidence suggests an increasing use of computers for training purposes, both as a means of simulation and as a medium for programmed learning.

5 *Wage and salary administration* – it is probably in connection with this area that EDP has been used for the longest period in personnel departments. As well as dealing with the routine of payroll calculation, ready analysis of data for costing, analysis and control purposes is available.

6 *Health and safety* – Statute law and insurance companies require that records of accidents be maintained; a simple task with EDP. Moreover, by analysing data, particular health or safety hazards or trends may be identified. Equally, the efficacy of preventative measures may be monitored.

7 *Labour relations* – while there is little evidence of its widespread adoption in the UK, it is apparent that in the USA both management and trade unions rely to a considerable degree on EDP data-banks, both as sources of information for negotiation and as means of developing models to test the consequences of proposals. Such use is so common that one American writer, with tongue firmly in cheek, has suggested that conventional negotiations be abandoned. In their place he suggests that both sides input their argument to a computer and allow it to work out the terms of agreement!

Recommended reading

Pigors, R. and Myers, C. A., *Personnel Administration: a point of view and a method*, McGraw-Hill, 1973 (Chap. 2).

Thomason, G. F., *A Textbook of Personnel Management*, 2nd ed., IPM, 1981 (Introduction).

Wille, E. and Hammond, V., *The Computer in Personnel Work*, IPM, 1980.

Watson, T. J., *The Personnel Managers*, Routledge & Kegan Paul, 1977.

Legge, K., *Power, innovation and problem-solving in Personnel Management*, McGraw-Hill, 1978.

Thurley, K., 'Personnel Management in the UK — A case for urgent treatment?' *Personnel Management*, August 1981.

Pratt, K. J. and Bennett, S. G., *Elements of Personnel Management*, Gee & Co. Ltd, 1979, (Chap. 1).

3 Human relations and work groups

Introduction

Despite the technological revolution to which industry is presently subject, work is still normally done in groups. A knowledge of how these groups function – group dynamics – is therefore essential if we are to understand worker behaviour. With hindsight, such a conclusion is obvious. It appears, however, to have been less obvious to the 'scientific school' of management theorists led by F. W. Taylor, who saw the worker as an essentially economically-motivated being. Almost by chance, one such theorist, Elton Mayo, stumbled upon the fact that workers were subject to a variety of group influences affecting motivation and productivity which could override basic economic considerations. This discovery is generally considered to be the starting-point of modern industrial sociology and, in particular, of group dynamics theory; a point amply reinforced by the frequency with which examination questions are either based on or refer directly to Mayo's work.

Sample examination question

Describe the characteristics a group should possess in order to maximise its work potential. Comment on the use of inter-group competition as a strategy for increasing organisational effectiveness. *(IAM)*

Key points

1 Group cohesion, the major determinant of group effectiveness. However, effectiveness not necessarily directed towards corporate goals.

2 Factors promoting/detracting from cohesion, eg size, homogeneity of membership, nature and arrangement of work, physical proximity, remuneration, style of leadership.

3 Cohesion often prompted by external threat or competition. Positive results of cohesion may potentially be stimulated by inter-group competition.

4 Competition also has negative consequences, eg distorted percep-

tion, hostility, lack of interaction and communication, all of which are potentially damaging.

5 Situation may be reached where one group 'wins' and another 'loses'. Tendency of winner to become self-satisfied while loser seeks scapegoat or commits himself to recouping the situation with potentially heightened inter-group tension.

6 Necessary for management to control situation. Possible tactics include identification of common goal/enemy, OD, emphasis on organisational interdependence, avoidance of win/lose situations, rotation of staff.

Suggested answer

Of the factors which determine potential group effectiveness both in terms of satisfaction and productivity, it is apparent that the most important is the degree of group cohesion. By cohesion is meant the degree of attraction that the group has for each of its members. It is of very real importance, therefore, that managers understand those factors which promote this feeling of group identity. At the same time, it must be noted that while a highly cohesive group may contribute very significantly to the achievement of corporate goals, so too it may exercise its strength against their achievement. The discriminating factor will be the extent to which the goals of the group synchronise with those of management.

Of the factors which promote cohesion, group size is of particular importance. While groups naturally vary in size, for successful interaction to occur a group must not be too large, (opinions vary concerning optimum size but somewhere between 5 and 9 appears to be the norm). In a large group individual deviance is more likely to be unnoticed or tolerated, thus detracting from commitment to group goals. Co-ordination also becomes more difficult as a group expands. In any case, as shown in Mayo's bank wiring room experiment, large groups tend not to survive – instead dividing themselves into smaller sub-groups. Generally, the more homogeneous the membership, the greater will be the level of cohesion, since conflict and competition is less likely to occur. Personal background, values and status should ideally match. Lack of homogeneity may, however, be tolerated where members' skills are perceived to complement each other, since in this way some equality of status may be established.

The manner in which work is arranged will also be instrumental in determining cohesion. Workers carrying out the same or similar tasks will tend to experience similar problems and stresses, thus establishing a common bond. Physical proximity will similarly encourage the development of a group identity. Where remuneration is based on group rather than individual performance, cohesion will be encouraged. Similarly, the organisational structure may stimulate conflict, thus hindering, if not precluding, the formation of close-knit groups. Particular characteristics of the occupation may also encourage group formation, danger or the antipathy of others solidifying group identity, eg miners or policemen.

The style of leadership adopted has also been shown to be a potent factor, though in two very different ways. It is generally accepted that a democratic, participative style will encourage cohesion and indeed may well assist in the integration of group and corporate objectives. At the same time, it is apparent that a group which feels itself threatened by an autocratic leader will close ranks to offer mutual protection against the common enemy. Such a reaction, indeed, is typical of any situation in which a group feels threatened by some external agency. This reaction has a valuable practical implication for management, since a similar reaction may be prompted by the use of inter-group competition. Research, in particular by Sherif *et al*, shows that, in a situation of inter-group competition, each group becomes more cohesive, better organised and more task-orientated, ie they become more productive.

At first sight, inter-group competition has thus much to recommend it. Regrettably, however, it is apparent that unless skilfully managed, less desirable results may occur. Increasingly, each group sees the other as an enemy. Both groups tend to develop distorted perceptions of themselves and the other group. A marked reduction in interaction and communication occurs, causing still further isolationism. Such effects could be highly damaging to the organisation. Ultimately, a position may be reached where a 'winner and loser' emerge. Schein suggests that while the winning group retains and may indeed increase its cohesion, it also tends to become more relaxed, complacent and often concerned for member needs rather than task accomplishment. The losing group may attempt to re-interpret the situation so as to escape admission of defeat or alternatively seek a scapegoat within or outside the group. Often it will re-examine its own performance in the light of defeat and seek ways of recouping the situation. This may be manifest in a total commitment to work harder, though often with even less inter-group co-operation than before, resulting in further tension.

Such competition, with all its consequences, is an innate aspect of man's humanity and may never, therefore, be totally eliminated. It is vital, however, that managers understand the problem and attempt to control the situation so that positive results outweigh the negative. Various tactics have been proposed to achieve this, the common emphasis being on co-operation and communication. A common goal or enemy may be identified. Organisational development techniques have been used with some success. Managers should take an active role in stressing the interdependence of groups within the organisation and may also promote inter-group communication. Rotation of group membership may be of value, while the avoidance of 'win/lose' situations will potentially do much to defuse the problem.

Further examination questions

1 What are the major influences on effective team behaviour?

(IOB)

2 Discuss the possible consequences of using inter-group competition as a means of increasing performance.   *(IAM)*

3 The Hawthorne studies are often quoted as the starting-point of

modern industrial sociology. What conclusions from these studies are relevant to the practice of personnel management today? (*ICSA*)

4 Discuss the major features and significance of EITHER
  i the Hawthorne experiments at Western Electric, OR
  ii the coal mining research of the Tavistock Institute in the 1940s in Britain. (*ACA*)

5 Comment on the extent to which an individual is influenced by his work group, and the implications this has for the administrative manager. (*IAM*)

6 What implications do you see for the management of personnel in the existence of an informal organisation alongside the formal structure as shown in organisation charts? (*ICSA*)

General comments on questions

Questions 1 and 2 between them require a selective re-iteration of the material covered in the suggested answer.

Questions 3 and 4 both invite initially descriptive reports of the work of Elton Mayo and/or Dr Eric Trist and K. W. Bamforth. If by this stage in your studies you are unfamiliar with either set of research, this should be remedied immediately by reference to the recommended reading listed below: both sets of research should be known *in detail*. A discussion of their significance is also required. Summarised very briefly, the results of Mayo's research suggests that:

1 The relationship between manager and subordinates is a determinant of performance. In the Telephone Relay study the workers concerned were made to feel important, consulted, given greater personal attention and freed from a former rigid and close style of supervision, ie a democratic or participative style of management was adopted.

2 Work is a social as well as an economic activity. Conceptions of workers as exclusively economic animals must be qualified. Matters of security and a sense of belonging are often more important than the immediate working environment.

3 Attitudes, and in particular attitudes to change, are determined not only by the technical nature of the change, but also by previous conditioning, both at and away from the workplace, and by the individual's role in the social organisation which exists at work.

4 A typical organisation consists of both formal and informal structures. Considerable influence is exercised over individual workers by the informal organisation. Codes of behaviour and group norms may exist with which the individual is required to comply – on occasions this may imply commitment to objectives incompatible with those of the employer.

5 Unofficial group structures, together with their goals and values, should be identified and taken into account if management is to successfully achieve corporate objectives.

Trist and Bamforth's later studies reveal very clearly the possible problems when attention is focussed on technical change without some attempt to consider the inherent sociological and psychological consequences. As a result of revised working arrangements, long-standing work groups and methods were disrupted with immediate and tragic effects on morale. However technically advantageous a structure or work system may be, it is of little value if rendered inoperable by the reaction of workers involved. Both technical and sociological systems must be seen as parts of an integrated whole.

Question 5 is concerned with the relationship between the informal organisation and the individual worker. Mayo's bank wiring room experiment reveals very clearly that informal groups develop both norms of behaviour and sanctions intended to ensure compliance. Membership of a group implies acceptance of both. From management's point of view, the most important of group norms is generally that relating to work control. Mayo's research showed that despite the existence of an incentive scheme, individuals adhered very closely to the informally determined level of output, despite the fact that higher earnings were well within the reach of all concerned. Such findings have been regularly confirmed, to the extent that at least one writer (Roy) who chose to research while working on the shop floor admits to having himself unconsciously complied with informal standards. Group pressure may cause attitudinal compliance. In his frequently quoted experiments, Asch demonstrated how individuals could be persuaded by group pressure to deny what they knew to be the truth. Language, clothing and a multiplicity of other modes of behaviour commonly signal acceptance of group standards and membership.

However, as might be expected, individuals vary in their degree of compliance with such norms. R. S. Crutchfield suggests that persons with above-average levels of intelligence, originality or self-confidence tend to withstand group pressure better than others scoring lower in respect of such characteristics. Situational factors are also relevant. In situations of uncertainty or threat, compliance is likely. Where goal achievement is dependent on group effort or where group goals duplicate those of the individual, conformity will again naturally tend to occur.

The implications of this for management have been touched upon already (see above). Management's attitude in our opinion should not be to attempt to crush the formation of such informal structures but rather to accept that informal and formal goals may be integrated. When this occurs, the informal structure is capable of making a very real contribution to corporate effectiveness. Achieving such a union is no easy matter and no guaranteed recipe for success can be provided. However, if such a recipe exists, it is probably to encourage the formation of a highly cohesive informal structure and then to seek to integrate it with the formal structure by participative leadership.

Whereas this question initially requires consideration of the relationship between the individual and the informal structure, **Question 6** requires an examination of the relationship between the informal structure and the formal. A good answer will discuss the existence of group norms, the possibility of conflict with formal objectives, and the manner in which formal and informal structures may be consolidated.

Recommended reading

Schein, E. H., *Organisational Psychology*, 3rd ed., Prentice-Hall, 1980 (Chap. 5).
Handy, C. B., *Understanding Organisations*, Penguin, 1976 (Chap. 6).
DuBrin, A. J., *Fundamentals of Organisational Behaviour*, Pergamon, 1974 (Chaps. 6, 8, and 10).
Pratt, K. J. and Bennett, S. G., *Elements of Personnel Management*, Gee & Co., 1979 (Chap. 2).

4 Motivation and job satisfaction

Introduction

A simple definition of a manager is 'a person who decides what has to be done, and then gets others to do it'. Clearly, therefore, motivation is fundamental to the successful completion of any managerial task whatever the discipline concerned. Its importance is reflected in the frequency with which it provides the basis for examination questions, and it is for this reason that we shall be dealing with two sample questions. Students studying for a wide range of professional and management examinations should be prepared to answer questions in this area, whether or not sitting specifically personnel management examinations.

The basis for successful answers to questions on motivation is undeniably a thorough understanding of generally acknowledged theories such as those propounded by Maslow, Herzberg, Vroom and McGregor. However, given that motivational theory is the focus of much current research, you should not be afraid to draw the examiner's attention to studies which conflict with or qualify such theories. It is also important that the subject is not considered solely at a theoretical level. Examiners will often wish to test your understanding of the practical implications of research. Ideally, in dealing with such questions you should draw from your own experience. At the same time, however, you should make sure that you are well acquainted with some of the better known published practical applications of motivational theory such as those introduced by Volvo, Philips or ICI. A particularly useful summary of such experiments is that of J. C. Taylor, which may be found in the Summer and Autumn 1977 editions of the IPM's *Personnel Review*.

Sample examination question (1)

'People only come to work for money.' Discuss. (*IOB*)

Key points

1 A commonly held opinion among 'traditional' managers, re-iterated by McGregor's 'Theory X' and Schein's 'rational economic man'.

2 Behavioural theorists have qualified this view: a brief description of the work of Mayo, Maslow, Herzberg.

3 A summary of techniques implementing such theories, eg management style, MbO, participation, job re-design. However, not all schemes have succeeded.

4 But some workers *are* principally motivated by money: the work of J. H. Goldthorpe.

5 However, variations are also apparent in connection with other factors, eg age, sex, job type. References to Vroom's expectancy theory, Adams's equity theory, McClelland's achievement motivation theory.

Suggested answer

Why do people come to work? In the opinion of many 'traditional' managers the answer is clear – people come to work to earn money. Money is seen as an all-important regulator, capable of determining precisely worker motivation.

Such attitudes are reflected in Douglas McGregor's 'Theory X', which describes man as disliking work and requiring coercion to put forth adequate effort. E. H. Schein suggests that managers frequently see workers as 'rational economic man', totally committed to economic gain and willing to be manipulated, motivated and controlled towards the achievement of that goal.

Such assertions must, however, be qualified both at an academic and a practical level. Elton Mayo in his Hawthorne studies demonstrated very clearly that work is both an economic and a *social* experience. One only has to study briefly the attitudes of redundant workers to appreciate that the desire for work is not exclusively based on economic need. The number of football-pools winners who choose to continue to work rather than live on their winnings similarly suggests that for many work has a greater significance.

Some insight into what motivates the individual is provided by A. H. Maslow. He argues that individuals have a hierarchy of needs, ranging from basic physiological needs such as food and drink to 'higher' needs such as status and ultimately 'self-actualisation'. Typically, the hierarchy is illustrated in the following form:

```
                    /\
      Self-actualisation needs
          /     |     \
     Esteem or status needs
        /       |       \
    Love or belonging needs
      /         |         \
   Safety or security needs
    /           |           \
  Physiological or basic needs
```

It is the satisfaction of such needs that motivates the individual. As one need is satisfied it ceases to motivate; but another higher in the hierarchy and as yet unsatisfied replaces it. In a development of Maslow's theory, Frederick Herzberg goes on to argue that money is not a motivator at all, but rather a 'hygiene factor' capable only of preventing worker dissatisfaction. According to him, it is factors such as achievement, recognition, intrinsic reward, responsibility and promotion which motivate. Two conclusions relevant to the question appear to follow from this research. First, it is clear that if money is a motivator, its potency declines sharply as basic needs are satisfied and higher needs, less easily economically satisfied, assume greater importance. It is also clear that if the individual worker is to be encouraged to work harder, it is most likely to be achieved not by monetary incentives, but by providing opportunities for the satisfaction of higher needs in the work-place.

Such opportunities exist in a variety of techniques and modes of management now in widespread use; for example, the adoption of participative management styles, management by objectives, and worker participation and consultation at a variety of levels. However, the proposition that has received most attention in recent years is undoubtedly job re-design. Job rotation is its simplest form. It involves training and moving staff from job to job at pre-determined intervals or at the initiation of the member of staff concerned, and has been used with success by organisations such as Polaroid. Job enlargement takes the process one step further: the task is broadened by adding on additional duties immediately preceding or following the current job. For example, in a number of its plants, the Philips organisation has replaced traditional mass production systems with schemes in which each shop-floor worker produces a complete product from the basic components. Job enrichment adds to completion of a task some aspect of management responsibility. Examples of its use are manifold, but undoubtedly the best known is that of Volvo, which combined the technique with group working arrangements. In each instance, the objective is the same: to build into a job opportunities for the satisfaction of social, esteem and self-actualisation needs, thus motivating the worker to the achievement of both personal and corporate goals. While many such experiments have been introduced with considerable success, it is apparent that others have failed. The reasons for failure are often obscure. However, some enlightenment may be achieved by reference to the growing body of evidence and argument which suggests that enlargement or enrichment is not desired by all groups of workers and that money may indeed be a prime motivator.

In a series of studies by J. H. Goldthorpe *et al* it became apparent that for many skilled or semi-skilled industrial workers work was an 'instrumental' activity, ie the workers concerned saw their jobs as means by which to earn money to achieve personal objectives away from the workplace. It can be argued that such instrumentality extends to all workers, since all must sell their labour. It is clear, however, that there is significant variation in the degree of importance attached to money by different worker groups. For some, particularly skilled or professional groups, work may become what Dubin calls 'a central life interest': a situation in which job and private life overlap or fuse. In such situations, money ceases to be an all-pervading preoccupation. Other studies have suggested differences in attitude to pay between the sexes, different age groups, and different job types, eg salesmen and engineers.

Such attempts to establish predictable correlations between individual characteristics and money motivation must, however, also be qualified. Vroom in his expectancy theory reveals the absence of a precise cause-and-effect relationship between money and job performance; other contextual factors intervene. He argues that the motivating force of money will be determined by the value that specific goals have for an individual and the extent to which he expects that money will be instrumental in achieving them.

Other theorists, eg Adams, argue that staff compare their income with that of others preceived to make a greater or lesser contribution to the job. Their perception of equity or otherwise determines their degree of motivation. McClelland in his achievement motivation theory suggests that the value of money is closely linked with an individual's need to achieve – the higher the achievement need, the lower the concern for reward.

From the above it seems probable that any attempt to define a simple relationship between worker expectation, attitude or degree of motivation and money is doomed to failure. On one hand there is a body of theory and research which suggests that as a motivator, the efficiency of money is severely limited. On the other hand, it appears that money's motivational potency is linked to a whole gamut of individual attitudes and expectations.

Sample examination question (2)

There is an opportunity for re-designing some jobs in your organisation. What factors would you consider before attempting such a task and what benefits would you hope to achieve?   (*IAM*)

Key points

1 No foolproof recipe for success exists; however, conclusions may be drawn from successful experiments.

2 Need to identify opportunities for job re-design: problems of cost both of introduction and operation.

3 How to re-design: possibilities are removal of controls, more meaningful packages of work, responsibility. Particular success with group schemes. Necessary to ensure feedback.

4 Important to consult with workers to ensure that change is desired. Worker skills or ability to receive training must also be considered. Scheme unlikely to be accepted unless 'hygiene factors' are satisfactory.

5 Early consultation with *all* staff involved is essential. The particular problems of junior and middle management: required both to introduce the scheme and modify their own role.

6 Plans must be made for re-equipment and re-training. Usual to introduce scheme on a phased basis to aid control.

7 Benefits of re-design: improved quality and quantity of output; enhanced morale, manifest in reduced absenteeism, turnover etc.

8 Benefits must be set against problems: cost, trade union resistance, worker resistance. Possible to over-enrich jobs so that frustration occurs.

Suggested answer

Although many organisations have experimented with job re-design, it is apparent that no foolproof recipe for success has yet emerged. In introducing such a scheme, therefore, the best that can be done is to draw conclusions from those experiments which have succeeded.

The starting-point for any such scheme is clearly to identify whether or not jobs exist which may be re-designed. All too often schemes are abandoned at this stage on the grounds that capital investment or the cost of negotiating the withdrawal of restrictive practices will be such as to render production cost uncompetitive. Certainly, available information suggests that this is a real risk: costs may indeed be higher than using conventional working methods. At the same time, it must not be overlooked that if the scheme succeeds, such costs are likely to be more than recovered by a more settled, enthusiastic and flexible labour force.

Having identified opportunities for re-design, the next question is how. Enlargement or enrichment may be introduced in a number of ways. Certain controls may be removed, the individual being given greater accountability for his own work. Work may be packaged so as to present a more natural or complete unit with which the employee may identify: additional authority may be given, or new and more difficult tasks allocated. Some of the most successful examples of re-design have been group-based, combining the advantages of enhanced individual motivation with those of group cohesion. In any case, caution must be exercised to ensure that the re-designed task promotes rather than hinders social relationships. Whatever the precise nature of the re-designed task, Hackman *et al* emphasise that it must be meaningful, the worker must feel personally responsible, and must be able in some way to determine what results he has achieved, ie there must be feedback.

Assuming that re-design appears possible, it is essential that account is taken of both the wishes and attributes of the workers concerned. It is, after all, they on whom the success or failure of the scheme ultimately depends. While change of any kind is rarely welcomed, care must be taken to discriminate between an anxious response to change and a real unwillingness to accept the proposed re-designed method of working. With some justification, it has often been argued that the need for enrichment is often more apparent in the imagination of academics and managers, resulting from their own perception of a 'boring job', than in the minds of those actually doing it. Account must also be taken of employees' ability to do the re-designed job, and ability and willingness to be re-trained. Reaction to re-design proposals has also been shown to be determined by workers' satisfaction with both the formal and informal work environments. If social or physical conditions or pay are unsatisfactory, re-design is unlikely to succeed.

It is apparent from existing schemes that the greater the number of staff involved as early as possible, the greater the chances of successful introduction and operation. Where they exist, trade unions will clearly need to be involved or at least consulted at an early stage. When planning consultation, it is important that junior and middle managers are not overlooked. Their role is particularly important, since it is upon them that the burden of introducing the scheme will normally fall. At the same time, they have often the most difficult psychological adjustment to make, typically relinquishing at least a part of their perceived managerial responsibility to the workforce, and often being required to assume the future role of counsellor rather than traditional manager.

Plans for re-equipment and re-training staff at all levels will be required. Normally, it will be prudent to introduce the new working method on a phased basis, thus allowing ease of monitoring and modification before more general application takes place.

So far as the benefits of such a scheme are concerned, these may be summarised as those which naturally occur when individual worker and corporate objectives are to at least some degree integrated. Results claimed include improved quality and quantity of output, a more flexible workforce, and improved morale, manifest in reduced absenteeism, labour turnover, labour relations difficulties etc. Such benefits must be seen in the context of the problems which commonly attach to the introduction of re-design. The problem of cost, both of introduction and operation, has already been mentioned. While not dismissing re-design totally, the reaction of trade unions is often hostile, as indeed may be that of managers and workers at all levels. It must never be assumed that all workers wish to participate in this way, or indeed consider it legitimate that they should be required to do so. A further problem is the risk that, in attempting to make jobs more demanding, they may indeed cause more worker frustration than before, with consequent management problems.

Further examination questions

1 'Not by bread alone'. Discuss in relation to employees' motivation to work. *(IOB)*

2 **a** What do you understand by 'job enrichment' and what do you consider to be its main advantages and disadvantages?

b Select a job in banking and show how it might be 'enriched'. Examine the effects of the changes you propose on other jobs and those who perform them. *(IOB)*

3 Discuss the contribution of one recent behavioural theorist to modern personnel policy. Illustrate by reference to the practices of an organisation known to you. *(ICSA)*

4 It is sometimes suggested that the attempts which have been made to incorporate the behavioural theories of motivation into managerial practice have been more acclaimed by the intellectuals than by the employees themselves. Discuss the view, illustrating your answer with examples. *(IAM)*

5 What is 'morale'? What is the precise relationship, if any, between productivity, morale and other indices of employee behaviour? *(ICSA)*

6 Explain whether or not you would expect the work motivation of

salaried staff to differ from that of wage-earning 'shop-floor'
workers.   (*ACA*)

General comments on questions

Question 1 is essentially the same as sample examination question (1), both in
content and emphasis.

Question 2 is intended to reveal candidates' knowledge of both the theory and
practice of job enrichment. Although the question asks for an example from
banking, it is clearly applicable to jobs drawn from other sectors of commerce or
industry.

In answering the question it is important to distinguish between job enlargement and job enrichment. *Job enlargement* involves the widening of duties by
adding new tasks to the existing job, making it less specialised and monotonous,
but without altering the degree of difficulty or responsibility involved. *Job
enrichment* extends a job not only horizontally, but also vertically by giving the
worker greater responsibility and the opportunity to make decisions and use
skills not previously employed. It is with job enrichment that this question is
concerned. The advantages and disadvantages associated with its introduction
have already been discussed in suggested answer (2).

So far as the effects of change on others are concerned, particular account
must be taken of management and supervisory staff, whose traditional role will
typically change to that of a counsellor with some loss of overt authority. Other
staff may be equally concerned because of fears of redundancy or because of the
disruption of social groups or long established work patterns. Workers engaged
in non-enriched jobs may also resent or doubt the legitimacy of the authority of
those carrying out enriched tasks, with inevitable conflict and non-co-
operation.

Question 3 invites you to select a theorist of your choice and demonstrate his
(or her) contribution to modern personnel policy. Although most students are
likely to opt for Maslow, Herzberg or McGregor, there is absolutely no reason
why some other should not be selected. Bear in mind, however, that the
examiner will require a fairly detailed description of his work, together with an
illustration of its practical implementation. In relation to all three theorists mentioned above, their contribution could be well illustrated by reference to an
organisation which has successfully introduced some form of job re-design.
Well known are experiments conducted by Volvo, ICI, Texas Instruments etc,
but again, you should feel free to give less well known examples, particularly if
these are drawn from your own experience. Reference should also be made to
the practical problems sometimes experienced when attempting to convert
theory into practice. Their precise nature will naturally be determined by the
proposals under consideration, but commonly include questions of cost and the
reactions of trade unions, staff and line management.

Question 4, despite its apparent anti-behavioural stance, requires a balanced
discussion of the reaction of workers to attempts to integrate motivational
theory into day to day management practice. As in Question 3 above, the
examiner almost certainly has job re-design in mind, but equally relevant are

worker reactions to management-by-objectives schemes or indeed to participative styles of management. The beneficial behavioural consequences of such schemes have already been discussed above. There is, however, a growing body of evidence which casts serious doubts on the general acceptability and effectiveness of job re-design techniques.

A feature of many experiments is that the re-design is only one aspect of the new working method. Other changes to pay and/or the work environment are often introduced at the same time. In such instances, it is clearly impossible to identify cause and effect with any degree of certainty. Hackman and Lawler argue that enriched jobs are attractive only to workers with strong self-expression and autonomy motives, while Hulin and Blood suggest that re-design is only appropriate to white-collar, supervisory and 'non alienated' blue-collar staff. Reference was made above (Suggested Answer (1)) to Goldthorpe's studies in the Luton area which revealed that many workers had predominantly instrumental or money-orientated attitudes and did not seek satisfaction of 'higher needs' at work. Nevertheless, it is at this type of worker that the majority of enrichment schemes are directed. The methodology of experiments claimed as successes has often been found to be less than satisfactory and indeed many of those employers who have succeeded with schemes of this kind have been those well-known for outstandingly good management/employee relationships. It is probably fair to say, therefore, that the case for enrichment is not yet fully proved or disproved.

Question 5 poses something of a dilemma, in as much as there appears to be no commonly accepted definition of 'morale'. Blum and Naylor suggest that it is 'the possession of a feeling, on the part of the employee, of being accepted and belonging to a group of employees through adherance to common goals', ie it is something very dependent on group membership. They go on to emphasise that it is *not* the same thing as job satisfaction. However, Guinon defines it as 'the extent to which an individual perceives that satisfaction as stemming from his total job situation'. Which is correct? We believe that a satisfactory definition lies somewhere between the two: morale is a product of individual job satisfaction and group cohesion.

So far as group cohesion is concerned, there exist generally acknowledged correlations. High levels of cohesion may generally be seen to result in reduced labour turnover, lower absenteeism and higher productivity where group and corporate goals are compatible. So far as job satisfaction is concerned, the picture is less clear-cut. There is evidence to show that high levels of satisfaction tend to be reflected in lower turnover, absenteeism and improved labour relations. Much management concern for worker satisfaction has rested on the assumption that a happy worker is a productive worker. Regrettably, there appears to be little hard evidence to support such a belief. Studies by Vroom, Herzberg and others have repeatedly failed to demonstrate any such connection. Indeed, there is an argument based on expectancy theory, that as job satisfaction increases, the value of extrinsic reward decreases, thus potentially reducing motivation and productivity.

In some instances, productivity may be high while job satisfaction or morale is low. In a highly automated factory where output is largely determined by the speed of the production line, productivity may still be high, even though many of the workers employed actively dislike their jobs. On the other hand, morale may be high, staff enjoying the work environment and the companionship of colleagues, while devoting very little time and attention to the job in hand. A more radical, but no less valid, proposition is that rather than job satisfaction resulting in high productivity, high productivity, in many cases, leads to job satisfaction. Management should perhaps, therefore, concentrate on emphasising productivity in the knowledge that high levels of morale are likely to follow, rather than occupying its time with attempts to make workers happier.

When considering what workers expect to derive from their job experience, one is constantly reminded that few irrefutable truths exist. This is the substance of **Question 6**. Many of the aspects of a good answer to this question have already been discussed in the suggested answer to Sample Examination Question (1) above. Reference was made to studies conducted by Goldthorpe *et al* in which were identified the instrumental attitudes to work held by many shop-floor workers. This was contrasted with Dubin's description of work as a central life interest for many skilled and professional working groups. Such attitudes are often the result of factors outside the organisation such as personal history, family influences and social class or aspiration. However, behaviour and attitudes are also moulded by intra-organisational factors such as technology, the limits and opportunities inherent in a job and the pervading style of management. The historical worker/staff distinction is itself potentially the source of differences in attitudes. Different ways in which 'staff' and shop-floor workers are remunerated, rewarded and treated on a day-to-day basis will often encourage the former to closely identify with the employer while further alienating the shop-floor group.

It is apparent, however, that employers are attempting to remove such differences. Job re-design (discussed above) clearly has as one of its goals the greater identification of even the least skilled worker with the organisation and its objectives. Other employers, eg ICI, are seeking to attack the problem by appointing all employees on a salaried staff basis, in the hope that this may lead to a more cohesive, co-operative, flexible and less status-conscious workforce.

Perhaps a less welcome indicator of the apparent unification of worker attitudes is represented by the growth of white collar unions. The increased size and complexity of organisations, the threat of new technology, and the erosion of differentials between blue and white collar workers have all contributed to the alienation of previously contented staff. In many areas of industry and commerce white collar staff appear to be adopting attitudes and tactics which mirror those of their blue collar colleagues.

Recommended reading

McCormick, E. J. and Tiffin, J., *Industrial Psychology*, George Allen & Unwin Ltd, 1975 (Chaps. 12, 13 & 16).

Goldthorpe, J. H. *et al*, *The Affluent Worker: Industrial Attitudes and Behaviour*, Cambridge University Press, 1968.

Taylor, L. K., *Not for Bread Alone*, 2nd ed., Business Books, 1980.

Schein, E. H., *Organisational Psychology*, 3rd ed., Prentice-Hall, 1980 (Chap. 4).

Lawler, E. E., *Pay and Organisational Effectiveness: A Psychological View*, McGraw-Hill, 1971.
Cooper, R., *Job Motivation and Job Design*, IPM, 1977.
Pratt, K. J. and Bennett, S. G., *Elements of Personnel Management*, Gee & Co., 1979 (Chaps. 2–4).

5 Manpower planning

Introduction

Manpower planning has been described by the Department of Employment as 'a strategy for the acquisition, utilisation, improvement and retention of an enterprise's human resources'. This definition gives an immediate impression of a wide-ranging and comprehensive activity. This impression is confirmed by fact. Those involved in manpower planning will need access to a great deal of detailed information and should be privy to the plans of the organisation for which they work.

It is essential to grasp from the outset that manpower planning is an integral part of the wider corporate planning activity. It is dependent upon, and in turn affects, other areas of planning, such as marketing, production and new technology. This interaction is illustrated by the diagram below. There is a constant flow of information and activity.

Manpower planning is, then, a continuous activity, not something which is carried out once a year, recorded, and tucked into a drawer. Although approaches vary, dependent upon the type and size of organisation, most manpower planning operations will involve:

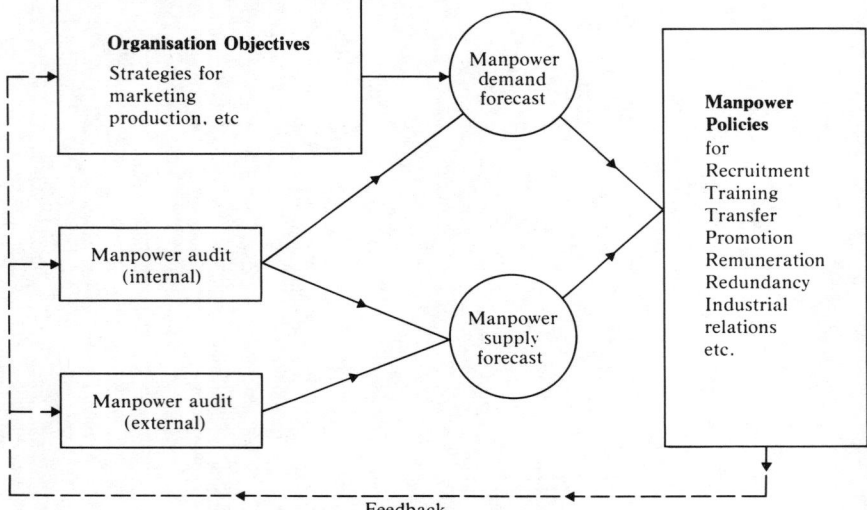

Fig. 5.1.   The manpower planning process

1 Setting objectives as part of corporate planning.
2 Carrying out an audit of existing manpower supply – both inside and outside the organisation.
3 Making forecasts of future supply and demand.
4 Modifying and implementing plans.
5 Controlling manpower levels.

It will be appreciated even from the above brief outline that manpower planning depends upon the cooperation and expertise of a great many people within an organisation. Although the Personnel Department will often be responsible for implementing and controlling the process, the total operation will involve managers and staff from various disciplines. Without a constant flow of both quantitative and qualitative information no manpower planning process would be effective.

From a practical commercial viewpoint there is a growing recognition in both the public and private sectors that the employment of individuals who are 'surplus' to the efficient running of the organisation is a luxury which could spell the difference between success and failure. If organisations wish to be competitive, they must plan and control their labour with the same degree of rigour as that applied to stock levels and capital projects. With the growth of legislation and other developments designed to protect the individual employee, the employment of permanent staff must be looked upon as a long-term decision. It is in this context that manpower planning takes on a sense of purpose which will appeal to even the most hard-nosed manager.

Examination questions relating either directly or indirectly to manpower planning appear regularly in most personnel management papers. They are usually of a 'general' nature but sometimes require knowledge of specific areas such as the analysis of labour turnover. Many of the general questions require sufficient knowledge to be able to enter into a discussion of the relevance and application of the manpower planning process to modern personnel management. We recommend that you keep abreast of current articles and comment in this area.

Sample examination question

> Can manpower planning ever be a precise process? If not, how can it assist management decision-making? (*IPM*)

Key points

1 Consider whether or not manpower planning can be a precise process in general terms. (Question gives a clear hint that it cannot.)

2 Deal with some of the specific problems besetting manpower planning which lead to lack of precision, eg poor information, lack of cooperation, volatile area.

3 Outline current context of management decision-making in organ-

isations – economic uncertainty; high cost of labour; social pressures; legislation; technology etc.

4 Highlight ways in which manpower planning can assist management by providing a basis for developing human resources to meet the future.

Suggested answer

Although techniques employed in manpower planning are constantly being improved, the overall process can be no more precise in an absolute sense than any other planning operation. Apart from the inherent problem of planning for contingencies, there is the added disadvantage of dealing with the most unpredictable of 'raw materials' – the human being. Apart from the need to produce statistical information and forecasts on staffing levels and movements, such things as skill, knowledge and motivation must also be assessed and, where necessary, improved. Manpower planning is not only concerned with quantities, it must also provide management with details of the quality and potential of the labour force.

It should be stressed that the manpower planning process can only be as good as the organisation's corporate planning operation. It cannot stand alone and relies greatly upon the co-operation and contribution of most areas of management. Its degree of precision will largely depend upon the reliability of its sources of information and the skill of those involved in analysing the data and making the forecasts. Much of the qualitative information will be obtained from line managers through such things as staff appraisal reports. It is in these areas that the subjectivity of human judgement affects the planning operation.

Whilst on the subject of constraint upon precision it might be appropriate to outline the context within which the modern manager has to make decisions. Despite the ability to produce and process huge quantities of data relatively cheaply, decisions, particularly those concerning the future, are still beset with uncertainty. Apart from economic uncertainty, there are the added problems of the high level of social change, often reflected in legislation, and the high cost of manpower together with a comcomitant shortage of skilled workers. Technological change also complicates the capital/labour mix and the speed at which staff need to be retrained or redeployed. These uncertainties, paradoxically, make it even more necessary to assess the present and plan for the future.

Given the above situation, how can manpower planning assist management decision-making? It should be made clear that decisions concerning manpower will be made with or without a systematic approach to manpower planning: it is the quality of those decisions which is important. Most strategic decisions will be based upon:

a An assessment of the present situation and how it was arrived at.
b A statement of what is to be achieved in future.
c A method of achieving the planned objectives.

Manpower planning can provide information for and react to this decision-making process.

In order to plan for the future management will wish to know a great deal about the numbers, ages, locations, pay, occupations, skills, knowledge, potential and ambitions of its existing workforce. It will also wish to know whether that workforce will be able to cope with the demands made upon it during the period of management's plans. If it cannot cope, where will staff of the right calibre be obtained and at what cost? Can they be developed from within the organisation or be recruited from outside? What are the industrial relations implications of proposed actions? These are the questions to be answered if management is to make informed decisions. It is these questions which manpower planning is designed to answer. As explained, some of these answers may not be 'precise' in any scientific sense, but without a systematic approach to manpower planning many would not be available at all and the quality of management decisions would suffer accordingly.

Further examination questions

1 Describe and discuss some alternative methods of measuring and analysing labour turnover, with comments on the main advantages and disadvantages of each. *(IPM)*

2 a *Some* labour turnover is unavoidable in all organisations. What possible benefits can this have?
  b What are the drawbacks of a very high turnover rate? *(CBSI)*

3 Discuss the place of manpower planning in a total personnel strategy. *(IPM)*

4 What are the problems of developing a manpower plan out of a corporate commercial plan? *(IPM)*

5 It has been argued that manpower planning, properly conceived and executed, is only worthwhile for organisations with more than 1,000 employees. How far would you agree with this assessment? *(ICSA)*

6 'Manpower planning is now the central aspect of the personnel function.' Discuss and account for the growing emphasis on manpower planning. *(ICSA)*

7 Describe the main phases involved in carrying out a company manpower plan for a five year period. *(IAM)*

8 If, as has been forecast, there is a stabilising (or even a reduction) in the number of building society branch offices in the future, what specific problems will be created for the personnel manager? What solutions can you offer? *(CBSI)*

9 Estimate the value of manpower planning in an organisation in today's environment. *(IAM)*

General comments on questions

Unlike the main question, **Questions 1 and 2** deal with the particular problem of labour turnover. Although labour turnover need not be linked with manpower planning, the analysis of turnover is a vital part of any manpower planning operation. There are two main parts to the analysis of labour turnover. Firstly, there is the question of collecting data and calculating quantities. Secondly, there is the qualitative aspect of investigating the reasons for staff leaving the organisation and endeavouring to reduce wastage where this is considered necessary.

Question 1 requires a knowledge of the mechanics of calculating levels of turnover, together with some criticism of the methods used. Most textbooks will include the most commonly used methods which would include:

a *The crude labour turnover index*

A percentage is obtained by dividing the number of leavers in the period by the average number of employees and multiplying by 100.

As the name implies, this index will probably need refining by applying it to categories of workers such as those employed in the same department or in the same occupation if it is to be useful to management. Apart from this it does not distinguish between wastage of long-term employees and turnover at the 'fringe'. For this we would need to employ:

b *The labour stability index*

$$\text{ie} \quad \frac{\text{No. of staff with 1 yr + service}}{\text{Total employed 1 year ago}} \times 100$$

This will inform management whether or not there is a high percentage of 'stable' employees unaffected by turnover.

Labour turnover can also be analysed graphically. Normally, curves are plotted over the period concerned indicating either the 'leavers' or 'survivors' of an entry cohort. 'Cohort analysis', as this method is called, is particularly relevant to organisations employing large numbers at any one time. These graphical methods are particulary effective for illustrating peaks or 'crises', as they are usually termed, ie periods of exceptionally high wastage. Examples of wastage and survival curves are given below.

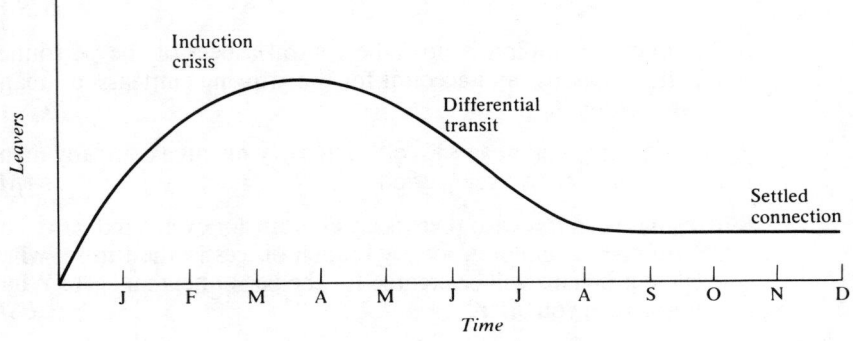

Fig. 5.2. A wastage curve, identifying three 'phases' as suggested by Tavistock Institute.

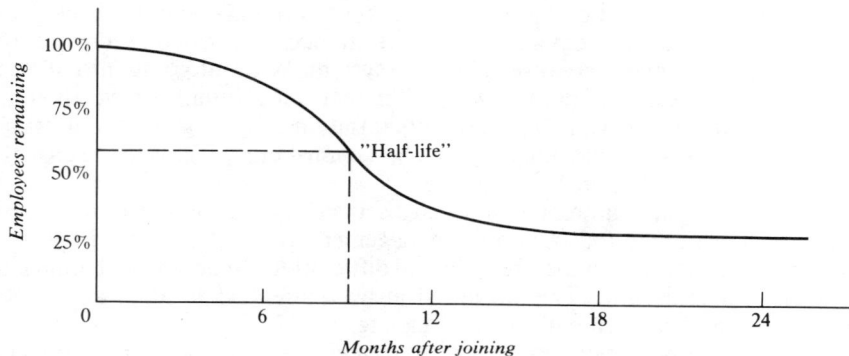

Fig. 5.3. A survival curve, showing time taken for 50% of entry cohort to waste.

Apart from the comparative advantages and disadvantages of the various methods of analysis, their common weakness is that they only provide quantitative information. In each case it would be necessary to find out the reasons for wastage if this was indicated to be of an unacceptable level.

Question 2 deals with the problems behind the levels of labour turnover but also requires a knowledge of the benefits. The main advantages of some turnover (bearing in mind that this may be virtually confined to death and retirement – often called 'involuntary' wastage) are 'new blood' and the ability to use natural wastage as an alternative to redundancy where circumstances dictate.

A good answer would include financial costs, ie those of recruitment, training, lost production, reduced quality and spoilage amongst the drawbacks of a very high turnover rate. It should also consider the 'social' costs of low staff morale and the public relations implications.

Questions 3, 4, 5, 6 and 7 are all 'general' questions on manpower planning approached from various angles. Much of the detail required for these questions appears in the Introduction and the suggested answer for the main question. There are, however, one or two specific points which need to be made.

Question 3 requires a discussion of the way in which manpower planning relates to personnel management overall. Although this will depend to some extent upon the degree of specialisation within the organisation, it is clear that manpower planning will form a central feature of a well-developed personnel strategy. It will provide the framework around which a great deal of activity will take place in respect of staff recruitment, development and deployment.

Question 4 deals with the development of a manpower plan. As stated, the manpower plan forms an integral part of corporate planning and would not exist without the latter. The relationship is a dynamic one and the problems of uncertainty and change have already been highlighted in the model answer. It is these problems which this question requires to be discussed in a realistic and practical manner.

Question 5 sets out to be provocative, but requires a well-balanced argument concerning the merits of systematic planning for the smaller organisation. The figure of 1,000 employees is somewhat arbitrary and the number of staff should not be the only criterion. The type of organisation and the environment in which it operates are equally important in deciding whether or not to incorporate a formal manpower planning system. Without going into all the arguments, it is probably fair to say that if manpower planning is a worthwhile operation, then it is worthwhile for all organisations. The degree of sophistication will, of course, vary, but it may well be a contributory factor to the growth of a small organisation into a large one!

Question 6 again requires an informed discussion of the relationship between manpower planning and personnel management generally. It also implies a realistic appraisal of both the strengths and difficulties of manpower planning in a modern organisation. The suggested answer offers some ideas and these should be supplemented with further reading.

Question 7 concentrates on the actual strategic operation of manpower planning over the longer term and the way in which it is carried out. Again, a knowledge of the relationship between manpower planning and corporate planning overall is required, together with an acknowledgement of the need to adjust constantly over such a period subject to feedback and revised plans. The multi-disciplinary nature of manpower planning will also need to be highlighted here.

A knowledge of the application of manpower planning to a practical situation is required by **Question 8**. Although the question appears specialised, it does in fact deal with the very problem which could confront any organisation. The point of the question is that effective manpower planning, linked to the corporate plan, will hopefully help management to avoid many of the problems before they arise. Remedies such as redeployment, natural wastage and redundancy would be amongst those employed to deal with this type of problem. Hopefully, the manpower plan would serve its purpose by avoiding the latter to any large extent.

Question 9 requires a similar treatment to that provided in the suggested answer to the main question.

Recommended reading

Bramham, J., *Practical Manpower Planning*, 2nd ed., IPM, 1978.

McBeath, G., *Manpower Planning and Control*, Business Books, 1978.

Company Manpower Planning, HMSO, 1974.

Bartholomew, D. J. (ed.), *Manpower Planning: Selected Readings*, Penguin, 1976.

Pratt, K. J. and Bennett, S. G., *Elements of Personnel Management*, Gee & Co. Ltd, 1979 (Chap. 5).

6 Recruitment and selection

Introduction

Recruitment and selection form a major part of the day-to-day work of many personnel departments. This is not to imply that these functions are the sole preserve of personnel management. In fact it should be stressed that although a great deal of the administrative and 'technical' load of the recruitment process is dealt with by personnel specialists, it would be absurd to exclude the line manager from this vital area.

The degree of the line manager's involvement will largely depend on policy and the wishes of the individual manager. In some organisations the recruitment of junior staff is left almost entirely to the personnel specialists, whereas more senior appointments will involve the line manager at all stages of the process.

The terms 'recruitment' and 'selection' themselves often cause confusion in the minds of students and this problem of definition does form the basis of some examination questions. Although difficult to generalise, it is probably fair to say that 'selection' forms part of the 'recruitment' process. Recruitment covers a variety of activities such as preparation of job descriptions and personnel specifications, advertising, processing applications, interviews and tests, placement and initial induction. It can be seen that the task of selection takes place at some point in this process but it is difficult to identify exactly where it starts or finishes. However, it is generally accepted that selection refers to the operation of actually 'choosing' from amongst a group of applicants, using one or more of a variety of available techniques.

Some writers do not favour the term 'selection' at all (see, eg, Torrington and Chapman) as they feel that it implies a one-way decision, ignoring the choice and free will of the applicant. This is an important point and has particular relevance when considering the selection interview, by far the most commonly used technique for selecting staff.

Sample examination question

'The reliability and validity of the interview is usually so low as to render it practically useless as a selection technique.' To what extent is this true? (*ICSA*)

Key points

1 Explain objectives of selection devices.

2 Necessary to define terms 'reliability' and 'validity' as applied to selection techniques and in particular to the interview.

3 Outline and develop arguments for and against the statement contained in the question in the light of research and practical considerations.

4 Balance evidence and form conclusions. Important to distinguish between effectiveness of interview as a predictor and its overall use as part of recruitment process.

Suggested answer

Selection techniques are employed with the objective of predicting the success or otherwise of an applicant for a job based upon certain criteria. The effectiveness of a particular technique will therefore presumably be judged by the extent to which it successfully achieves this objective.

The selection interview has been the subject of extensive criticism despite its central position in the selection procedures of the vast majority of organisations. Much of this criticism is aimed at its actual effectiveness as a selection tool rather than its overall benefit as part of the recruitment process. Foremost amongst the critics are those who advocate 'objective' selection techniques such as psychological tests. Amongst the most vociferous of the advocates of the 'scientific' approach is H. Eysenck, who regularly criticises interviewers for failing to set criteria in respect of job success or for not pursuing criteria in the interview.

Criticism of selection techniques is usually divided into two aspects – 'reliability' and 'validity'. The reliability of a predictor (in this case the interview) normally refers to its ability to measure different candidates in a consistent way against specified criteria, or alternatively, to produce similar results in respect of a particular candidate when administered by different persons. Much research over the years has concluded that many interviewers fail to agree on the evaluation of the same candidate. This has led reviewers such as Morgan to reach conclusions similar to those stated in the question. However, Rodger and Munro Fraser are among leading advocates of the reliability of interviewing based upon thorough preparation and a structured approach.

The validity of the interview is, like any selection device, judged by the extent to which it is able to predict success or failure in the job. Here again the work of Kelly and Fiske and many others has thrown doubt upon the interview's ability to identify candidates who would succeed in the job concerned. Much of the research has highlighted the problem of subjectivity, inherent in many interviewers. However Vernon's research into Civil Service selection found that the interview, when conducted by experienced and fully trained personnel, compared favourably with other selection techniques. It would seem that, as with reliability, the argument revolves around the quality of the interviewer rather than the interview itself. This point appears crucial to any consideration of the interview's effectiveness.

The subjectivity or bias displayed by many interviewers is, to many critics, the central weakness of the technique. Problems of 'halo effect' – the favourable quality of a candidate which overshadows other faults – are well known. 'Stereotyping', whereby the interviewer attributes to an individual traits which are commonly associated with persons of his physical appearance, background or whatever, is another commonly quoted example of subjectivity. It is difficult to deny that all individuals possess certain attitudes or prejudices and that these will often affect the judgement of an interviewer. The degree to which he is able to control or even ignore these when assessing a candidate will undoubtedly affect the effectiveness of the interview.

Given the above arguments, what conclusions can be drawn and what can be done to avoid future criticism? The review of research findings by Carlson *et al.* probably provides the most positive guidance in this respect. It is suggested that, *inter alia*;

- Structured interviews are more reliable and valid than unstructured ones.
- Interviews should form part of an overall selection procedure and be supported by other techniques as appropriate.
- Interviewers should receive intensive training.
- Feedback on the results of interviews is necessary if prediction is to be improved.

In conclusion it should be stressed that the prediction of human behaviour is fraught with difficulty and all selection techniques have strengths and weaknesses. The latter are likely to be most evident when techniques are employed by the untrained and inexperienced. The statement made is probably true of the worst interviews but can be improved upon by thorough training and preparation. Finally it should be remembered that the interview provides the vital opportunity for the candidate to make his own prediction concerning the potential employer!

Further examination questions

1 Discuss the criticisms which have been made of the interview as a selection tool and describe how you would set out to make the interview process less open to criticism. *(IPM)*

2 The interview can often be an inaccurate selection technique. How can its accuracy be increased, both by the improvement of the interview itself and by the use of additional techniques? *(IAM)*

3 Describe what you understand by the recruitment, as distinct from the selection, process. *(IPM)*

4 What contribution can a recruitment specialist make to the selection of staff in a highly technical function of which he has only a limited amount of knowledge? *(IAM)*

5 By what means can the cost-effectiveness of recruitment policies and procedures be assessed? *(ICSA)*

   6 Should psychological testing play a greater part in management
   selection in this country?   (*IPM*)

   7 Describe the main types of selection tests and outline their uses in
   recruitment in the building society industry.   (*CBSI*)

   8 Describe the essential steps in employee selection. Write a short
   paragraph to explain each step.   (*IOB*)

General comments on questions

Questions 1 and 2 are similar to the sample question dealt with above, although
Question 2 will require a discussion of the use of techniques such as testing and
group selection, referred to elsewhere, as a supplement to the interview.
   Question 3 is on matter discussed in the Introduction to this section.
   Question 4 begs the question of the utility of the specialist knowledge of personnel managers. The examiner appears to require a discussion of the ways in
which the line manager with technical job knowledge and the recruitment
specialist might co-operate in order to improve the selection process. As discussed, selection is not the preserve of the personnel specialist and technical
criteria can only be prepared with the assistance of line management. It is likely,
in fact, that the line manager will make the final decision. It is in the area of
choosing appropriate selection techniques and of acquiring suitable skills that
the recruitment specialist can make the greatest contribution.
   Despite the fact that John Courtis has written a book entitled *Cost-Effective
Recruitment*, **Question 5** is the type of examination question which has no
specific or quantifiable answer. The financial cost of recruitment can be
calculated reasonably accurately by costing staff time spent on preparation of
job descriptions, personnel specifications, preparation of advertisements, dealing with applications, interviewing etc. To this could be added direct costs of
advertising, agency fees and so on. There will also be the indirect costs of poor
recruitment which results in high turnover, lost production and wasted training
costs. It is probably the need to reduce the amount of recruitment to a minimum
which lies at the heart of this question. Subject to external pressures on turnover, this will depend on ensuring that the right persons are selected in the first
place by thorough preparation and the effective use of selection techniques. The
cost-effectiveness of recruitment procedures can only be achieved in the light of
continuous feedback as to whether or not we are matching individuals to jobs
sufficiently well to avoid costly duplication of effort. Having assessed effectiveness under some financial criteria, it will also be necessary to consider the largely
unquantifiable damage which poor recruitment can cause in terms of morale,
productivity, etc.
   Question 6 deals with the use of psychological tests as techniques of selection
with particular reference to management posts. It is probably fair to say that
tests are now used in this country to a greater extent than ever before. This
should not imply that they begin to approach the usage of the selection interview. Whether or not psychological tests should be used more widely depends
upon their effectiveness in predicting the particular criteria connected with the
job in question. We return to the problems of reliability and validity which have

been discussed in the main question concerning the interview.

Although proponents of selection tests refer to their 'objectivity', this is of little use if they do not predict the qualities which we are seeking in the candidates. Although the reliability of some tests appears fairly high, there are doubts amongst many practitioners regarding what they actually measure. Psychological tests can be extremely attractive, particularly for those attempting to assess things such as intelligence and personality. However, the many tests available are a minefield for the unwary and inexperienced and it is generally accepted that they should only be used as part of a wider selection procedure rather than on their own. Acceptability of selection techniques on the part of the candidate is also an important consideration and some individuals may react negatively if they are unable to appreciate the relevance of a particular test. Holdsworth's short booklet on selection testing, details of which appear in the recommended reading, is strongly recommended for guidance.

Question 7 also deals with selection tests and requires knowledge of the different types in use. A list of the more readily available tests would probably include:

1 Skill tests – both practical and written.
2 Aptitude tests.
3 Intelligence tests.
4 Trainability tests – which have become increasingly popular in recent years – basically test an individual's ability to learn and benefit from training.
5 Personality tests.

Although it is likely that building societies, in common with many other organisations, do not use selection tests widely, it would not be difficult to think of areas in which they could be used when considering the wide spectrum of staff which many societies employ.

Although **Question 8** draws upon much of what has been written above and is a straightforward question, it requires a knowledge of all the essential stages of the *selection* process (as opposed to *recruitment*). Answers will need to describe clearly and comprehensively the considerations and activities involved. A sound treatment would include:

- Preparation: need for recruitment (manpower plan); job analysis; job description; person specification.
- Attracting applicants: advertising; application forms; short-listing.
- Selection techniques: interviews; tests; group selection; etc.

The examiner would appear to expect all of the above aspects to be included but this question poses, once again, the problem of deciding what activities are regarded as 'recruitment' and what as 'selection'.

Recommended reading

Ungerson, B., *Recruitment Handbook*, 2nd ed., Gower Press, 1975.
Shouksmith, G., *Assessment Through Interviewing*, 2nd ed., Pergamon, 1978.
Fraser, J. M., *Employment Interviewing*, Macdonald & Evans, 1978.

Holdsworth, R. F., *Personnel Selection Testing – a Guide for Managers*, BIM, 1972.
Forbes, R., 'Improving the Reliability of the Selection Interview', *Personnel Management*, July 1979.
Gill, D., 'How British Industry Selects its Managers', *Personnel Management*, September 1980.
Pratt, K. J. and Bennett, S. G., *Elements of Personnel Management*, Gee & Co. Ltd, 1979 (Chaps. 6–9).

7 Staff appraisal

Introduction

Though prophets of doom have been repeatedly foretelling its demise, studies of staff appraisal practice reveal that its use is increasing. This increased use is reflected in its frequent selection by examiners. It is a subject that crops up not only on personnel management papers, but also with unfailing regularity on general management papers of the kind set by many professional bodies.

Used for many years in its 'merit-rating' form, appraisal has often been considered merely a means of determining salary or wage rises on an 'objective' basis. Current practice suggests an awareness of its wider potential as a means of motivation and a tool of management information and control. Indeed, many organisations now choose to separate totally appraisal from salary determination.

Sample examination question

Organisations are increasingly using performance appraisal schemes. What do you think are the essential elements of an effective appraisal scheme?

In your answer, mention especially:

a The objectives of the scheme;

b The mechanics of the scheme, including your views on who should carry out the appraisal and who should receive the information resulting from the appraisal. (*ICSA*)

Key points

1 A brief statement of what is understood by the expression 'performance appraisal schemes'.

2 The objectives of such schemes, subdivided into two categories: those dealing with the provisions of management information and those relevant to motivation.

3 A summary of the mechanics of a typical procedure.

4 A more detailed description of a typical method with references to alternative methods and the need to avoid problems of subjectivity.

5 A brief discussion of questions associated with the appraisal interview: why managers often wish to avoid it; the style to be adopted.

6 Who should appraise? While typically carried out by the immediate superior, a number of organisations have experimented with alternatives, eg subordinate, colleague, self-appraisal. Important to distinguish between self-appraisal and the increasingly used pre-interview self-assessment.

Suggested answer

Although appraisal of staff strengths and weaknesses occurs as a crucial part of any manager's or supervisor's daily task, recent studies show that an increasing number of organisations are choosing to complement such informal appraisal with formal staff appraisal procedures. The term staff appraisal in this context means the evaluation of the performance and/or potential of existing staff. It is also frequently referred to as merit-rating.

The objectives of appraisal schemes fall into two principal categories: those concerned with the provision of management information, and those which seek to motivate. Information gathered provides the basis for manpower planning and subsequently contributes to corporate planning by identifying areas in which the organisation has a ready supply or shortage of staff of a particular kind or with particular skills. Such data is vital for recruitment purposes and in avoiding or minimising the need for or consequences of redundancy. Where weaknesses are apparent, training, and in extreme cases, disciplinary action may be required. Under-utilised skills or aptitudes may be identified, prompting promotions or transfers to the mutual benefit of employer and employees. Typically, data collected provides a basis and reveals the need for salary reviews. The effectiveness of other personnel procedures such as recruitment and training may be verified against the ultimate criterion – performance; while at the same time providing feedback allowing the development of perhaps more accurate criteria against which to measure predictors.

So far as motivation is concerned, appraisal constitutes a potentially major stimulus. For many employees the simple awareness that their efforts will be scrutinised regularly by management will be enough to urge them to greater efforts. Others, appreciative of its further ramifications, will see it as an opportunity for reward through increased salary, promotion or improved job satisfaction. In an otherwise hectic daily round, the appraisal interview may present the employee with an all too rare occasion when his superior takes time to discuss with him his current role and aspirations. In short, the objectives of staff appraisal relate to all aspects of personnel management activity.

Most schemes follow a similar pattern, ie:

1 A report is prepared on each employee to be appraised. Usually this takes place once or twice a year.

2 Each employee is interviewed.

3 Appropriate follow-up action is taken as determined by the report and interview.

Many kinds of appraisal method are available. More traditional methods, eg ranking, linear scale, paired comparison, forced distribution, require the appraiser to evaluate employees against certain predetermined criteria or each other. Behavioural techniques, eg critical incident, forced choice, emphasise employee behaviour in specific circumstances. Management by objectives (MbO), involving appraisal against objectives mutually set and agreed by manager and subordinate, is also used. Of such methods, the most common is probably the linear scale method.

For each employee to be appraised a form is provided listing a series of factors or characteristics, eg quality of work, quantity of work, initiative, co-operation. Against each factor is a scale on which the appraiser is required to indicate his assessment of the employee in respect of that factor or characteristic. As with most methods it is particularly useful when based on performance and thus criteria capable of measurement rather than traits of a less tangible nature, since in this way problems of subjectivity may be minimised.

The appraisal form completed, the next step in the process is perhaps the most contentious: whether or not the contents of the form should be discussed with the employee concerned. Arguments against discussion usually pivot around managers' dislike of appearing to 'play God' in conducting the appraisal interview. They argue that such situations will often produce inhibited reports consisting of platitudes and things that the subordinate would like to hear rather than accurate assessments of strengths and weaknesses. Research partially supports such a view. However, without honest and open communication of management's attitudes and ideas, the productivity of appraisal is drastically reduced. How can an employee be motivated to work harder or improve if he is not aware of management's opinion of his abilities? Equally, account must be taken of the effect of non-communication. An appraisal system, hidden from the eyes of all but a senior few, shrouded in mystery, is unlikely either to instil confidence or improve morale. Rather it may provide a breeding ground for all manner of gossip and rumour, often of a highly personal and disquieting nature. Recent surveys suggest that the majority of managements, appreciative of such problems, do reveal the content of forms, at least in part.

Following the interview and completion of any remaining portions of the appraisal form, appropriate follow-up action is taken. As discussed earlier, this typically involves arrangements being made for training, promotion, transfer or improved remuneration. Studies of appraisal procedures suggest that in the majority of schemes, appraisal is carried out by an employee's immediate superior. Since he will have day-to-day experience of the employee concerned, this is wholly reasonable. However, alternatives have been suggested and indeed introduced to a limited degree. A number of major organisations have, for example, experimented with colleague appraisals, arguing that these are often more accurate, revealing and acceptable than those made by superiors. Appraisal by groups of supervisors have been used in an attempt to overcome problems of individual subjectivity. In a number of schemes the initial report is reviewed by a senior member of management who also conducts the appraisal interview. A more radical proposal employed by the US armed forces involves appraisal by subordinates -- not surprisingly perhaps, this has met with little popular support. Equally limited in application, it would appear, is the idea of self-appraisal. However, the use of a modified form of self-appraisal, the use of self-assessment as the basis for joint appraisal, is becoming more common. An essential part of a growing number of schemes is the preparation by each employee of a personal assessment prior to the appraisal interview. Proponents of such an arrangement suggest that in this way the interview ceases to be a situation in which the superior tells the subordinate about his strengths and weaknesses, becoming instead a more constructive, less defensive and more meaningful method of improving mutual job satisfaction and performance.

Further examination questions

1 Describe the objectives of performance appraisal. How would you carry out the performance appraisal of a subordinate? *(ICSA)*

2 What are the advantages a manager could expect to achieve by regularly appraising the work performance of his subordinates? *(ICSA)*

3 Staff appraisal has many different purposes. Specify the main purposes and describe ONE method of staff appraisal which you think most likely to achieve these purposes. *(IAM)*

4 'Staff appraisal is a time-consuming administrative chore.' How would you attempt to convince company middle management of the true value of a suitable appraisal scheme? *(IAM)*

5 Why do performance appraisal schemes so commonly run into difficulties? *(IPM)*

6 Assess the validity of the reasons usually advanced in favour of a formal, systematic appraisal scheme. Why is an effective appraisal scheme so difficult to achieve in practice? *(ICSA)*

General comments on questions

While **Questions 1–4** above are essentially very similar to the sample examination question both in content and emphasis, **Questions 5 and 6** require altogether different treatment. **Question 5** requires that you deal exclusively with the problems of staff appraisal; and **Question 6** that you balance the benefits accruing from such schemes with their associated difficulties. What are these problems?

1 Fundamental are the problems of reliability and validity. Both have already been discussed earlier when considering selection techniques. By validity is meant whether or not the interview measures what it is supposed to measure: by reliability, the extent to which the interview would yield the same results time and time again if applied to precisely the same circumstances. Both are

essential if the interview is to have any real purpose – both are notoriously difficult to prove.

2 Perhaps the problem most associated with appraisal schemes is subjectivity. This manifests itself in a whole variety of forms, of which the more common are:

    a *The halo effect and stereotyping*: a particular characteristic displayed by a member of staff leads the appraiser to be biased favourably or unfavourably in assessing other aspects of performance.

    b *Constant error*: certain appraisers will regularly give high ratings, others regularly low ratings; creating problems when attempting to make comparisons between staff appraised by different appraisers.

    c *Central tendency*: a common tendency among appraisers is not to use the full range of values on the appraisal scale, but to group all staff in a narrow band, often 'average' or 'above average'. While this may reflect the true state of affairs, it is often a reflection of the appraiser's reluctance to 'judge' subordinates. Equally, of course, it may reflect his lack of any real knowledge about them.

    d *Recency*: assessments are made on the basis of easily remembered events or behaviour immediately preceding the appraisal, rather than over the full period in question.

3 Negative appraiser and/or employee reaction to the appraisal procedure is clearly a major problem. Reference was made in the suggested answer to appraisers' common discomfort in appearing to 'play God' – often reflected in the lack of objectivity with which they approach the task. Understandably, the reaction of staff to appraisal is often hostile. For some it may appear an artificial and unnecessarily formal interruption to a good day-to-day relationship with their superior. More typically, however, it is an experience approached with nervousness often resulting in defensive unwillingness to participate fully in the procedure. At best it may elicit a stereotyped, uninformative response.

4 In many cases, points or values are attached to factors against which staff are to be appraised. This is particularly common when appraisal results are to be used for salary administration purposes. How the points are allocated is a potential source of distortion. Not only can distortion arise out of comparatively incorrect values being attached to characteristics or modes of behaviour, but also from the spread or cluster of ratings. Generally, the more widely spread the ratings in respect of one factor, the greater will be that factor's real rather than intended value. While such problems may be eliminated by lengthy statistical process, very often the determination of values is a hotch-potch of guesswork and compromise.

5 Lack of senior management commitment to appraisal is regrettably a common obstacle to success. All too frequently appraisal forms are filled, filed and forgotten – promises of follow-up action made to staff are similarly forgotten. All too often appraisal is something to which junior staff are subjected in the knowledge that their seniors will escape a similar experience. Any initial confidence in or enthusiasm for such schemes is understandably soon eroded.

Such problems severely limit the usefulness of appraisal schemes. They may, however, be controlled, at least to some degree.

1 If the commitment of all staff is to be maintained, this must be established early on by involving as many staff in the planning of the scheme as possible. Often this will require the involvement of trade union representatives. The scheme must also be seen to be applied to all staff, irrespective of status.

2 Training can do much to overcome many of the problems outlined above. Training of appraisers will assist in developing an awareness of and thus consideration of problems of subjectivity, as well as how to best handle the appraisal interview to derive optimum mutual satisfaction and benefit.

3 The design of the method and procedure to be adopted should, while achieving its purpose, be as simple as possible. Often the confidence of those required to operate the scheme is lost through what appears to them to be an irrelevant and unreal display of expertise by the personnel department. Again such problems may be reduced by participation in the scheme's preparation and planning.

4 Management must be seen to take appraisal results seriously. Employees who feel unfairly treated should be allowed the opportunity to state their case or appeal. Follow-up action, once promised, should be implemented or an explanation given for failure to do so.

Recommended reading

Randell, G. A., Packard, P. M. A., Shaw, R. L. and Slater, A. J., *Staff Appraisal*, IPM, 1974.

Beveridge, W. E., *The Interview in Staff Appraisal*, George Allen & Unwin Ltd, 1975.

Gill, D., *Appraising Performance: Present Trends and the Next Decade*, IPM, 1977.

Levinson, H., 'Appraisal of What Performance?', *Harvard Business Review*, Vol. 54, No 4 (July-August 1976), pp. 30–40.

Pratt, K. J. and Bennett, S. G., *Elements of Personnel Management*, Gee & Co. Ltd, 1979 (Chap. 10).

8 Training and management development

Introduction

Training has become a major growth industry in recent years. The government continues to pump ever-increasing sums of money into industrial training through the Manpower Services Commission, quite apart from the huge investment in training by industry. Countless courses and varieties of training are available from establishments in both the public and private sectors, in addition to in-house activities. Against this background and rising unemployment, the demand for workers with suitable skills is, paradoxically, as strong as ever. Organisations require managers and workers who are able to employ the latest techniques and technology in order to ensure success. In view of the above it is hardly surprising that training and development form the subject of many examination questions.

It might be appropriate at an early stage to clarify any confusion concerning the terms 'training' and 'management development'. Training can, of course, cover a whole range of knowledge and skills and various techniques can be employed with all levels of staff. 'Management training', in our view, forms part of a much wider process known as 'management development'. The latter will attempt to prepare managers for future challenges as well as equiping them to fulfil their present roles effectively. It will involve various activities which are referred to below, but adequate training forms an important part of any development programme.

Examination candidates should be prepared for questions concerning the 'institutionalised' side of industrial training and should possess adequate background knowledge of developments in this area. Knowledge of the workings of the Manpower Services Commission and the Industrial Training Boards is an obvious example. A thorough understanding of what might be termed 'the training process' is also essential. Here, we are concerned with the functional side of training – the planning, doing and reviewing process. It would be difficult to structure an answer to a question on these aspects of training without some framework upon which to build. There is a tendency to advocate a 'systematic' approach to training, which although apparently rather mechanistic, does provide a logical approach which can be readily understood by the layman. A typical graphical presentation of the systematic approach is given overleaf.

This diagram illustrates clearly the major stages of the operation and stresses the continuous flow of activity which takes place in training. The feedback of information is an essential part of the process, which adjusts accordingly.

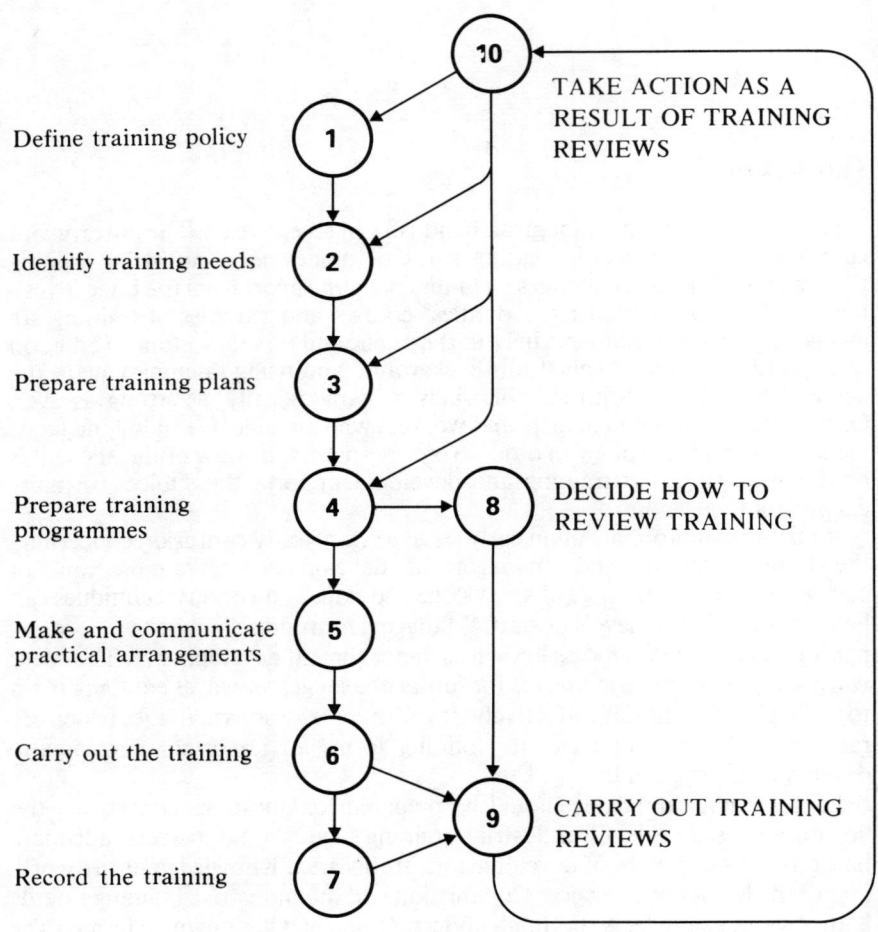

Define training policy

Identify training needs

Prepare training plans

Prepare training
programmes

Make and communicate
practical arrangements

Carry out the training

Record the training

TAKE ACTION AS A
RESULT OF TRAINING
REVIEWS

DECIDE HOW TO
REVIEW TRAINING

CARRY OUT TRAINING
REVIEWS

Fig. 8.1.   A systematic approach to training (By permission of HCITB)

In view of the above approach it would probably be wrong to talk about a 'beginning' and 'end' to the training process. However, many questions appear to ignore the 'doing' part of training and concern themselves with the identification of training needs, ie the start of the process or the evaluation of training which tends to take place at the end. Students should therefore ensure that they understand the theory and practice of these particular aspects.

Questions on management development usually require an appreciation of the place which training plays as part of a development initiative and the types of training available for staff of this calibre. They will, however, demand a wider understanding of development techniques, including such things as job rotation, projects, coaching and MbO, as well as the need to allow for responsibility and scope in the day-to-day work of the manager.

Sample examination question

The identification of training needs is the first stage of any systematic training programme. What are the ways in which these needs can be accurately identified? *(CBSI)*

Key points

1 Stress difficulty of identifying needs on a once-and-for-all basis. Need for flexibility and adaptation to change.

2 First stage – to analyse organisation's present position and objectives – identify problems which might be solved through training initiative. (May require other solutions.)

3 Second stage – analyse jobs and work demands.

4 Third stage – assess performance of current staff – staff appraisal techniques etc.

5 Compare present performance and knowledge with that required by individuals and organisation and assess whether 'gap' can be filled through training.

Suggested answer

There is no simple way of identifying training needs, as these are arising and changing all the time. Neither is there any all-embracing exercise which will solve the problem at a stroke. This is not to say that training needs should be left to chance and dealt with on an *ad hoc* basis. Most organisations will wish to build up an assessment of both overall and individual training needs in order to set priorities and make the best use of available resources. This will almost certainly imply a flexible rolling plan which could be modified in accordance with particular pressures upon the organisation and its staff.

If the identification of needs is to be at all systematic, it will almost certainly start with a review of the organisation's objectives and its present position. Where a manpower planning process is in operation, this should provide much of the information concerning the ability of the work-force to cope with the present demands and those of the future. This review should reveal a combination of general and individual training needs, but might also offer alternative means of meeting problems such as a change in recruitment policy or the re-design of jobs. It should also highlight areas which require general training input due to such things as changes in government policy or legislation.

At the individual level it will be necessary to analyse the skills and knowledge required for the various jobs within the organisation. Apart from the usual job description form, it is essential to break down the skills, knowledge and responsibilities involved and to develop some criteria of performance. This operation, including an assessment of the changing demands of the job, should indicate what is required of the job-holder, and to some extent the ways in which he may learn the skills and knowledge required.

The second stage of this level of the analysis will inevitably be an assessment of the staff concerned with a particular view to training needs. Having assessed the demands of the job, it will be necessary to compare these with the performance of present incumbents. In practice, performance can be measured according to various criteria and by several means including tests, observation and other forms of appraisal. Some formal staff appraisal schemes do not make adequate use of the appraisal interview for the assessment of training needs and the individual concerned is often the best judge of any inadequacy which may be impeding performance.

Having assessed the demands of jobs and the performance of those employed in the context of the organisation and its environment, it should be possible to identify training needs with some accuracy. However it must be recognised that the theory will be subject to a great many practical and human problems. Research has shown that a great many organisations determine their training 'needs' in accordance with the whim of management based upon social or political considerations.

A realistic approach to the identification of training needs would incorporate much of the above but would almost certainly be integrated with other management activities such as manpower planning, staff appraisal and reporting systems on such things as productivity, absenteeism and wastage. In this way training becomes a natural part of the overall management activity and links in with other methods of dealing with needs at both the organisational and individual levels.

Further examination questions

      1 How would you set about an analysis of training needs in an organisation?   *(IPM)*

      2 Outline what you understand by the systematic approach to training, and show how it is (or could be) applied with regard to a specific category of employee.   *(ICSA)*

      3 Describe the steps involved in conducting a cost-benefit analysis of a training programme and outline the major difficulties that you would encounter.   *(IPM)*

4 Assess the contribution of the Industrial Training Board system to the improvement of industrial training over the last 15 years. *(IPM)*

5 In what ways have learning theories contributed to the techniques of training? Illustrate your answer with examples of how these theories have been applied in particular training courses. *(CBSI)*

6 What is the difference between 'training' and 'development' when these terms are incorporated in such phrases as 'management training' and 'management development'? *(ICSA)*

7 What part should training courses play in management development programmes? *(ICSA)*

General comments on questions

Question 1 covers similar ground to that of the main question, although it implies greater emphasis upon the individual's approach to the analysis of training needs.

Question 2 requires knowledge of the 'systematic' approach to training which was referred to in the introduction to this section. The diagram should prove useful to candidates attempting this question. Personal experience would be useful in applying this approach to a specific category of employee, but it should not be difficult to follow through the 'planning – doing – evaluation' process for (say) a group of supervisory staff requiring training in interpersonal skills. Needs might be identified indirectly through communications problems or poor industrial relations, or directly through appraisal of the supervisors. Skills will have to be analysed and programmes arranged, followed by a suitable form of evaluation (see below) which would be used to modify future training where necessary.

Question 3 does in fact deal with evaluation of training although using the term cost-benefit. It is appropriate that candidates are asked to refer to 'major difficulties', as this is one of the most notoriously difficult areas of training. Large organisations spending many millions of pounds each year on training admit that they have no watertight method of assessing the cost-benefit of this effort. As Hamblin points out in his excellent book, many organisations seek to judge training against financial criteria but soon realize that relating training directly to profits is extremely difficult. He talks about different 'levels' of evaluation and relates in his Chapter 5 how anyone wishing to evaluate training on a cost-benefit basis cannot avoid using intermediate criteria such as the effects of training upon learning and job behaviour. Hamblin advocates the selection of appropriate evaluation criteria for the type of training being undertaken. As he states, 'We can say that the real (or ultimate) objective is the maximisation of profits; but it is useless to state this as an evaluation criterion if we cannot obtain the information on which we can judge whether profits rose as a result. . . .'

Question 4 should only be attempted by those who have either had experience of, or read fairly widely about, the ITB system. Apart from background reading in personnel management texts, it is necessary to keep abreast of developments through articles in publications such as *Personnel Management* and the *BACIE Journal*, in addition to press reports.

Question 5 requires knowledge of the theory behind the techniques employed in training. Candidates are recommended to obtain a grounding of the work of leading psychologists in this area and the principles of learning which have been developed. For example, they should be familiar with the following:

a Motivation is a pre-requisite for optimum learning to take place.
b Reward will stimulate the trainee.
c Knowledge of results or feedback is most important.
d Reinforcement will often assist learning.
e Learning by doing may be most effective for some trainees.
f The transfer of training to the job is a critical consideration.

Many of the above principles have been derived from the concepts of 'drive – stimulus – response – reinforcer' which are admirably dealt with in Bass and Vaughn's book, recommended below.

Questions 6 and 7 deal with management development generally as well as training for managers. As mentioned in the introduction, management development involves a wide range of activities, including various types of training. It is the relationship between development and training which these questions require to be explored. It would be all too easy to fall into a semantic argument on this subject and it is probably true to say that definitions of 'management development' vary and change with time. There is at present a trend away from individual development towards 'organisation development', which involves the wider team-building aspects of management. (See Section 17 on 'Change and Organisation Development').

In attempting to specify fundamental differences between 'training' and 'development' in this context, it is probably fair to say that training involves increasing competence in a specific role whereas development is concerned with skills and knowledge required for future roles and situations. Apart from the techniques mentioned in the introduction, training courses do play an important part in any development programme. Courses will range from short in-house up-dating sessions to external residential courses designed to develop inter-personal, leadership and decision-making skills. It is, however, important to remember that many consider development to be a matter for each individual and that he is often the best judge of his needs. All this points to a balanced programme taking into consideration the needs of the individual, the management team and the organisation.

Recommended reading

Hamblin, A. C., *Evaluation and Control of Training*, McGraw-Hill, 1974.
Bass, B. M. and Vaughn, J. A., *Training in Industry: The Management of Learning*, Tavistock, 1973.
Roberts, T. J., *Developing Effective Managers*, IPM, 1974.
Singer, E. J., *Training in Industry and Commerce*, IPM, 1977.
Pratt, K. J. and Bennett, S. G., *Elements of Personnel Management*, Gee & Co Ltd, 1979 (Chaps. 12–13).

9 Job evaluation

Introduction

From an examination point of view, job evaluation may arise in a direct type of question requiring an overview of the subject. Alternatively, knowledge of the utility and techniques of the process may be required in order to tackle questions which, on the face of it, are not to do with job evaluation. It is necessary, therefore, to have clear ideas about the scope and limitations of job evaluation and its relationship to other activities.

Apart from the actual techniques used to evaluate jobs, there are certain principles which all students should grasp before embarking upon detailed study of the subject:

1 Job evaluation sets out to assess the *relative worth* of a group of jobs.
2 It is only concerned with *jobs*, not the *individuals* doing them. Individual performance must be rewarded separately.
3 Although it adopts a *systemmatic* approach, it is not scientifically accurate and relies upon human judgement to a greater or lesser extent.
4 *Actual* pay levels can only be fixed through bargaining and market forces; job evaluation is concerned with differentials and the production of a structure of pay rates.
5 A job evaluation exercise can only apply to a particular point in time and structures will require revision and eventual overhaul.

If students are able to appreciate the objectives and limitations of job evaluation and apply these to practical problems, they will undoubtedly find it easier to understand the detailed operations involved. Most schemes are introduced in response to a pay system which has become chaotic due to various historical pressures and 'patching-up' exercises. It is to restore some semblance of order to this situation and introduce a 'fair' structure that most job evaluation schemes are initiated. In fact, an overriding consideration for an acceptable scheme is that it is seen to be fair by those affected.

In an age of growing trade union and staff participation, it goes without saying that any management contemplating job evaluation would do well to consult staff and their representatives at an early stage. It is quite common to have staff representation on the panel set up to assess the jobs under evaluation and where the workforce is unionised there will undoubtedly be a fair amount of negotiation taking place throughout the exercise.

Further detail will be introduced in the course of the examination questions which are considered below. However, many students find difficulty in grasping the application of job evaluation. The actual schemes carried out by various organisations are reported in articles and journals from time to time and these are recommended as a method of getting the process into perspective.

Sample examination question

What are the advantages and limitations of job evaluation as a way of settling problems of wage differentials?   (*ICSA*)

Key points

1 Define 'differentials' and compare with internal and external 'relativities'.

2 Outline types of problem which could arise concerning differentials.

3 Explain advantages of employing job evaluation as a means of coping with these problems – systematic and 'fair' approach.

4 Deal with limitations, eg subjectivity, market rates, anomalies, collective bargaining etc.

5 Summarize arguments for and against and draw conclusions.

Suggested answer

Wage differentials is the term normally used to describe the pay differences within a particular group of employees. This may be contrasted with the 'relativities' which may exist between different bargaining groups within a single organisation or between the employees of one organisation and those of another. The separation of pay relationships into differentials and internal and external relativities as defined by the Pay Board in its 1974 Report may seem somewhat pedantic. However, this demarcation is relevant to the limitations of job evaluation and will be referred to below.

Problems of wage differentials can arise in various ways. They normally occur over a period of time and may be due to such things as technological change, the bargaining 'muscle' of a particular group or *ad hoc* arrangements by a harrassed management. The end result will be differentials which are not considered 'fair' by many of those affected.

Job evaluation is a method of restoring some order and fairness to this situation. The BIM has described it as 'a process of analysis and assessment of jobs to ascertain reliably their relative worth, using the assessments as the basis for a balanced wage structure'. Through the use of a systematic and open approach it should help to:

a Establish *acceptable* differentials as part of an equitable pay structure.
b Create a pay system which is easier to understand.
c Assist industrial relations by reducing grievances over relative wages.

d Provide a framework into which new jobs can be fitted as they arise.

The actual process of job evaluation can also provide unexpected advantages. The need to review and produce current job descriptions may itself highlight operational problems concerning job relationships, not to mention inadequacies in respect of recruitment and training. It may also present an ideal opportunity to extend consultation with the staff and provide them with the opportunity to participate in a major project. These factors will increase the chances of success in overcoming the problems of pay differentials.

The above comments might give the impression that job evaluation is a 'cure-all' which should be used on every possible occasion. Unfortunately this is not the case and as with most schemes it has its limitations. As stated, job evaluation deals with the *relative* values of a series of jobs. It cannot determine actual levels of pay, which will be affected by market rates and collective bargaining. Neither can it provide for individual merit or effort – only the *job* is evaluated and individual rewards must be dealt with separately.

The other main weakness of job evaluation is the inevitable subjectivity which permeates the process. Very few, if any, schemes are able to ignore the *status quo* and the various political pressures within an organisation. Fairness will be diluted with a variable degree of pragmatism and bias.

Despite the gap between the ideals and reality of job evaluation, it still has much to commend it as a means of settling the problems of wage differentials. Provided it is conducted in an open manner, in close consultation and co-operation with the staff and their representatives, it will provide an acceptable framework upon which to build a pay structure suited to the needs of the organisation and its employees.

Further examination questions

1 Discuss the strengths and weaknesses of job evaluation. *(IPM)*

2 What are the possible advantages to an organisation of introducing a job evaluation scheme for manual jobs, and what are the likely and possible limits to the utility of the scheme? *(IPM)*

3 Is job evaluation the answer to the central problems of wage and salary determination? *(ICSA)*

4 What do you consider are the main objectives of any payment scheme? In your opinion what is the best way of achieving these objectives? *(CBSI)*

5 To what extent is the points method of job evaluation useful in establishing the basis for factory pay scales? *(ACA)*

General comments on questions

Question 1 is quite similar to the main question above and is dealt with in the suggested answer and the introduction.

Question 2 also requires similar treatment although it is slightly more specific. The reference to manual jobs might imply greater emphasis upon the potential industrial relations benefits through a scheme which is introduced with union co-operation. Reference might also be made to the ability to update job descriptions and take account of technical change. The limits to the utility of a scheme have already been referred to in the main suggested answer – ie that it will only provide a framework at one point in time and despite the ability to make adjustments, it will not avoid the perennial problems of collective bargaining and the market place.

Question 3 continues in the vein of critical analysis of job evaluation. The unwary candidate could fall into the trap of exulting the wonders of job evaluation as a 'cure-all' for the problems of determining wages and salaries. However, the question requires a well-balanced discussion of the benefits of a sound job evaluation scheme, together with its limitations (which have been well aired above).

Unlike the questions discussed above, **Question 4** takes an indirect approach and is only partially concerned with job evaluation. Some candidates may, in fact, fail to appreciate that it requires a knowledge of job evaluation at all. The objectives of a payment scheme are dealt with elsewhere in this book, but would include:

a The attraction and retention of staff;
b The motivation of the workforce;
c To minimise anomalies and disputes arising therefrom;
d To create scope for progression within the organisation;
e The creation of a structure which is seen to be fair as regards reward for the job and pay differentials.

There are various ways of achieving these objectives (also dealt with in more detail elsewhere) which would include:

1 Constant research into such things as labour market conditions, inflation and other trends;
2 Regular consultation and negotiation with staff and/or recognised trade unions;
3 Introduction of suitable incentive schemes;
4 A carefully structured reward package which includes fringe benefits;
5 A well designed pay structure based upon job evaluation with provision for review and up-dating.

Although this question extends well beyond a knowledge of job evaluation schemes, those who either lack this knowledge or fail to appreciate its relevance would be missing a vital ingredient.

Question 5 is more specific than the other examples in that it requires a knowledge of job evaluation methodology. It is fortunate that it refers to what is probably the most common method employed. Students often find confusing the wide choice of systems available. This is hardly surprising when many of them appear unduly complex, not to mention dubious, even to the professional. The more common systems tend to be discussed as two groups – the 'non-analytical' and the 'analytical'. The former group includes such methods as ranking and job grading which tend to possess the virtue of being simple to understand. However, they are sometimes considered too simple to deal with more complex organisations and this is where an analytical system might be preferred.

The points method of job evaluation is an analytical system which relies upon a detailed job description for all jobs under consideration. Points are awarded to each job based upon pre-determined criteria or factors, eg skill, experience etc. It is a systematic approach which endeavours to reward all aspects of a job and, because of its basic logic and attention to detail, it is considered to be strong in the 'seen to be fair' area. For those not familiar with points rating, as it is commonly called, we strongly suggest immediate reference to the reading list below.

This question requires application of knowledge of points rating to a factory situation. The main points to concentrate on will be methods of job analysis, a suitable choice of factors and the choice of 'bench-mark' jobs. Emphasis will also need to be given to the need for close consultation with trade unions throughout the scheme and their probable inclusion on the evaluation panel. The establishment of a hierarchy of points and the building of a suitable structure will also be dealt with, together with the negotiation of pay rates and the handling of anomalies and appeals.

Recommended Reading

Walker Morris, J., *Principles and Practice of Job Evaluation*, Heinemann, 1973.

ACAS, *Guide No. 1: Job Evaluation*, HMSO, 1976.

Livy, B., *Job Evaluation: A Critical Review*, Allen & Unwin, 1975.

Job Evaluation, BIM, 1961.

Thomason, G., *Job Evaluation: Objectives and Methods*, IPM, 1980.

Pratt, K. J. and Bennett, S. G., *Elements of Personnel Management*, Gee & Co. Ltd, 1979 (Chap. 14).

10 Rewards and incentives

Introduction

The subjects of financial reward and the administration of pay systems provide a fruitful source of examination questions. The range of questions is so wide, in fact, that we have decided to provide two sample examination questions and suggested answers in this section.

You must be prepared to deal with questions ranging from the direct 'Write all you know about salary administration' type to more subtle questions which require discussion of principles in a particular context. In order to bring some order to bear upon this confusing array of questions, it might be helpful to attempt to analyse the main areas of knowledge required. The following would appear to be the major areas of concentration:

1 Incentive theory – money and motivation.
2 The social connotations of 'wages' and 'salaries'.
3 The principles and practice of salary administration.
4 Wage payment systems – their relative merits and disadvantages.
5 Fringe benefits and their place in the reward package.
6 The economic and political factors affecting pay.

Many questions will, of course, require a knowledge of more than one of the above areas and in varying degrees. However, if you do not have a reasonable knowledge of any of the above areas, you should remedy this before the examination. General knowledge should be reinforced with specific detail of relevant research and practical examples wherever appropriate.

Sample examination question (1)

What factors should be taken into account when determining salary scales for managers? (*ACA*)

Key points

1 *Policy* – competitiveness; 'fairness'; reward for effort; progression.

2 *Objectives* – based upon overall policy, highlight particular objectives and methods of achieving them. Importance of consultation at this stage.

3 *Structure* – choosing an appropriate salary structure based upon the organisation's objectives and the aspirations of the staff.

4 *Review* – the need for regular review of salaries, both overall and for each individual – current practice (fringe benefits).

5 *Control* – the need for financial control and methods of achieving it.

Suggested answer

The factors to be taken into account when determining salary scales will ultimately depend upon the overall ethos of the organisation and its policy on salaries, assuming it has one. Any well managed organisation will have made policy decisions concerning such things as 'fair rates of pay'. This 'fairness' will need to embrace such things as competitiveness with similar organisations and the relative worth of jobs within the structure. Despite the debates concerning money and motivation, the reward of individual effort might well be a consideration and most organisations would wish to provide scope for salary progression in line with career development. Although policy statements are sometimes considered to be rather vague and irrelevant, this need not be the case. They should give a clear lead to those administering the salary scheme regarding the views and priorities of senior management.

Before determining the actual salary scales, specific objectives should be considered and set. These will be based upon policy and might include the following:

a *Regular research into market rates of pay*
If staff are to be attracted and retained, this knowledge is essential and should be linked to the review process (see below).

b *A system of job analysis and evaluation*
In order to determine internal relativities on a 'fair' basis it might well be necessary to review all job descriptions and carry out a job evaluation exercise. Where the pay system has grown up on a haphazard basis, this step, although time-consuming, would be an essential foundation for the design of suitable salary scales.

c *A structure which provides for suitable career progression*
Any salary scale should provide sufficient range and scope for individuals to progress in accordance with their particular aspirations and abilities.

d *The regular review of individual performance and salary based upon a staff appraisal scheme*
A formal system of staff appraisal is often considered to be the fairest way of reviewing the performance and contribution of individual members of staff. This is often used as a basis of assessing any increment over and above any cost of living increase.

The formulation of the above objectives and their implementation must take place in an open and consultative climate. Any salary administrator who fails to consult the managers concerned will be storing up problems for the future. Increasingly, middle management is being represented by trade unions and it is important that they be involved in the planning and implementation of the above activities.

The choice of a suitable salary structure will also depend to a great extent upon the type of organisation and its overall philosophy, together with the nature and aspirations of its staff. The types available range from the most rigid, based upon age and service, to the more flexible which allow considerable latitude within an overall framework.

It has already been stated that a good salary structure will be based upon sound job evaluation. This will usually provide data on the range of jobs to be included in the system and a grading system can be constructed around these. Areas for consideration will be the number of grades, the range of each grade, the degree of overlap between grades and the number of incremental points in each grade (assuming an incremental system is employed). Although most systems employ a series of overlapping grade boxes, these variables determine the final structure. The number of grades will to some extent be determined by the number of 'job families' identified and the range and overlap will attempt to accomodate various levels of performance and progression. Organisations based upon a strict hierarchical structure may prefer defined incremental points within grades, whereas other organisations may prefer the flexibility of free movement within grades. The latter systems are usually referred to as merit salary scales and are often geared to the appraisal system referred to above.

Having decided upon a structure, it is vital that it is constantly updated in line with such things as inflation and market rates. This overall review should be taking place in parallel with the individual reviews referred to. Salary administration is a dynamic process and it must react swiftly to economic and social pressures. This will include the need to take a modern view of fringe benefits, which cannot be ignored when considering the rewards of managers (an area too complex for discussion in detail here).

Any organisation operating a major salary and fringe benefit package must incorporate a system of financial control. The ability to pay is a crucial factor for the survival of the organisation and, without going into detail, strict controls and budgets must be implemented for such things as overall manning levels, re-gradings and merit increases. A loose salary system may spell financial crisis for many organisations, particularly those in labour-intensive sectors of industry.

The determination of salary scales for managers brings into play a complex network of factors. The above discussion should highlight some of the more important considerations.

Sample examination question (2)

What are the economic and other advantages of 'payment by results' wage systems? Have they a future?   (*ICSA*)

Key points

1 Definition of 'payment by results' (PBR) systems and variations found in practice.

2 Economic arguments in favour of PBR systems.

3 Operational advantages and disadvantages of PBR schemes.

4 Considerations when deciding whether to use a PBR system.

5 The future of PBR wage systems.

Suggested answer

'Payment by results' (PBR) wage systems of various kinds have been in use for many years. As the name suggests, they are based upon the rationale that workers will produce more work if payment is directly geared to effort. Over the years there have been many variations based upon this premise, designed to achieve economic advantages whilst at the same time attempting to avoid some of the operational problems referred to below.

One of the simplest and easily understood methods of PBR is individual straight piecework. Under this system the individual worker is paid in direct proportion to the amount of work which he produces, based upon an agreed rate per 'piece' of work. Due to pressures from 'indirect' workers such as maintenance engineers and other variations in individual operations, many piecework schemes have been organised on a group basis.

Apart from piece rates, there are systems based upon time-saving, such as the Halsey Plan and the Bedaux Point Scheme, whereby standard job times are calculated through work study and savings shared between employer and employee on an agreed basis. Similarly, schemes such as the Emerson Plan employ 'efficiency' percentages and pay bonuses for performance above an agreed level of efficiency. The latter has been widely used for both manual and clerical workers in the nationalised electricity supply industry.

Other schemes rely upon wider measures of performance which often embrace all the staff of a plant or company. Some, such as the Scanlon and Rucker plans, pay an annual bonus based upon a suitable index such as increase of productivity or labour cost/earnings. Profit-sharing bonus schemes are employed by many organisations such as ICI, Boots and John Lewis, and although there is a certain PBR element within these systems, the relationship between reward and effort is usually considered to be rather remote.

The economic arguments in favour of PBR systems are relatively straightforward from the employer's point of view. By inducing a worker to increase his performance beyond the norms achieved without incentive, the employer can maintain his standard unit costs and at the same time improve his overhead recovery rate. This is particularly true of 'job and finish' schemes. Apart from the more obvious fixed overheads such as rent, rates, heat and light, the costs of supervision may also be drastically reduced due to the self-motivating effects of the scheme upon the worker.

The theoretical economic benefits of a PBR scheme can often be successfully transferred to the operational situation and provide concomitant advantages for the workforce. Operatives will have greater freedom over their pace of work and their earnings will be related to their effort, often enabling them to increase pay in absolute terms. However, where either technical or social conditions are less than ideal, many of the economic advantages for both management and workers may disappear.

The well-known experiences of the Bank Wiring Room at the Hawthorne Works have been replicated many times and are reflected in the empirical research of people such as Roy and Whyte who spent much time in industrial situations. The central problem of group piecework has been well summarised by Lawler and Porter. They state that where workers mistrust management, high output will be restricted by fears of management action leading to rate cutting and/or redundancy. As a result, group norms will be set for output levels and pressure brought to bear upon those who deviate from the norm. It certainly seems to be the case that the overall climate of mistrust surrounding the fixing of standards and the measurement of work is at the centre of the failure of many PBR schemes. Company-wide schemes appear not to suffer so much from these problems but meet other difficulties with regard to the calculation of bonuses by often complex formulae.

In view of the operational difficulties referred to, are the economic benefits of sufficient magnitude to induce management to use a PBR wage system? The following are among the necessary considerations:

a Is high output of greater importance than quality?
b Does the workforce prefer stable earnings or high, but possibly fluctuating pay?
c Do production methods lend themselves to a PBR system, eg do workers have sufficient control over output?
d Is there a negotiating procedure which is sufficiently sophisticated to deal with regular pay rate bargaining?
e What is the industrial relations climate and structure like within the organisation?
f Are pay systems in different departments compatible or will there be work-flow problems?

During the 1950s and 1960s PBR systems fell into disrepute, due largely to the operational and industrial relations problems referred to above. Many organisations turned to systems such as Measured Daywork, which provides the advantage of a sustained 'high' level of output and pay without the fluctuations and uncertainties of PBR. However, there has been a revival of interest in PBR systems in some industries and schemes based upon larger work units appear to be favoured. Nevertheless, increased automation will preclude some of the more traditional forms of PBR and it is likely that there will be a move towards plant-wide bonuses and profit-sharing schemes.

It is suggested that there is no perfect wage system. PBR may be eminently suited to one organisation but disastrous for another. Each organisation will need to analyse its own circumstances, possibly based on Lupton and Gowler's well-known 'matrix' system. After carefully considering such things as the technology employed, the labour market, nature of the workforce and bargaining procedures in existence, management can decide whether PBR wage systems are appropriate.

Further examination questions

1 What are the key characteristics of a sound company salary scheme? *(ICSA)*

2 In what ways might production bonus schemes for factory staff act as a disincentive to greater productivity? *(ACA)*

3 What considerations should a personnel manager bear in mind in trying to select wage payment systems for a particular organisation? *(IPM)*

4 It is often the case that some building societies pay their staff higher rates of pay than do other building societies. Outline objectively the reasons for this. *(CBSI)*

5 Discuss whether individual Branch Office costings should be taken into account when determining the salaries of the Manager and his staff. *(CBSI)*

6 What is the distinction between 'wages' and 'salaries'? Discuss the implications of the distinctions which you make here. *(IPM)*

7 What are fringe benefits? Why do organisations provide them, and what useful purpose do they serve in practice? *(ICSA)*

8 What do you understand by the phrase 'employee benefit package'? Identify four major employee benefits and explain what incentives they offer to employees. *(IOB)*

General comments on questions

Question 1 is a straightforward question on salary administration and the suggested answer for Sample Examination Question (1) would be appropriate.

Question 2 is of a type extremely popular with the examiners of professional bodies and is partially dealt with in the suggested answer to Sample Examination Question (2). The question refers to the paradoxical situation whereby, given a poor industrial relations climate, a financial incentive scheme will produce below possible levels of output. Candidates should be familiar with some of the huge amount of empirical research which has been carried out in this area and be able to explain clearly how restrictions on output occur. Whyte's book (see reading list), although somewhat dated, clearly illustrates the situation.

A more general question on wage systems is provided by **Question 3**. Some of the considerations have been referred to in the suggested answer to Sample Examination Question (2) above. Lupton and Gowler's book is the definitive work in this area (see recommended reading), and although their 'matrix' system might frighten off some readers, the overall approach is to be recommended. Angela Bowey's article in the April 1976 edition of *Personnel Management* also gives a good overview of pay systems. Lupton and Gowler suggest that there are

four groups of influences that affect the operation of payment schemes:
- Technology;
- Labour market;
- Disputes and disputes procedures – number and length of stoppages etc;
- Structural characteristics – eg number of job grades, labour cost as percentage of total costs, bargaining arrangements.

It is not possible to discuss these in detail here but it is for each organisation to analyse its own position in these areas and design a pay system which fits its own particular circumstances.

Question 4, although referring to building societies, is basically concerned with the variations in pay between one organisation and another. Candidates are required to explain the economic and practical reasons for this. Many of the possible reasons are quite logical but require some thought. The following are some suggested areas which could be explored:

Ability to pay – are surpluses available for higher pay?

Willingness to pay – what are directors' views on staff salaries?

Unionisation – Is there an effective trade union or staff association?

Job titles/duties – Are rates of pay for similar work being compared?

Efficiency – Do some societies expect more work per person?

Overall reward package – Do working conditions vary?
                                – What about fringe benefits?

Size/Place – Is society based in 'high cost' inner city area?
              – Do responsibilities vary with size of organisation?
              – Are there economies of scale?

Many of the above considerations could equally apply when comparing the pay of organisations in other sectors of industry and commerce.

Question 5 is somewhat specialised but also contains certain principles concerning pay. It is to some extent an 'advantages/disadvantages' type of question which requires a treatment of both the commercial and human aspects. There are obvious attractions of incentive and efficiency from a management point of view and one could envisage a climate of cost-cutting within many branches. However, on the basis of branch comparisons one could envisage certain inequities which any costing system might import. The size and geographical position of the different branches must be an important factor and much would depend on the items of expenditure which branches would have to bear. Dependent upon the proportion of salaries affected by the scheme, fluctuations in salary may lead to insecurity and many of these types of scheme do not accurately reflect the efforts of staff. They are also open to abuse and 'fiddling'. The question is, of course, indirectly concerned with the motivational effects of monetary reward and knowledge of research could be brought to bear.

Question 6 is concerned with the distinction between wages and salaries referred to briefly in the introduction. One can get into a semantic argument but the common usage may be employed to discuss the differences. The following points should be included in a discussion of this type, some more obvious than others:

a Frequency and method of payment.
b Incentive elements and earnings curves.
c Fringe benefits and overall reward value.
d The social and industrial relations aspects.

Candidates should be aware of trends towards 'staff status' for the employees of many organisations, of which ICI is a prominent example. The effect of the distinctions upon attitudes should also be illustrated and the work of Goldthorpe *et al* and Lockwood would be useful references in this respect.

Questions 7 and 8 are concerned with the wider aspects of employee rewards. Fringe benefits have become an important consideration in recent years for both employers and employees. It has been estimated that employee benefits account for at least 30% of the payroll of larger organisations, and employees expect their employers to offer a benefit package which is in line with current practice. Over the years many benefits such as pensions, paid holidays and sick pay have been taken for granted by employees and they would not consider them to be 'fringe' benefits. The current range of 'perks' available goes far beyond the commonplace for some levels of employee. These receive a fair amount of publicity from time to time and we do not intend to go into detail here.

Many benefits have been introduced in order to overcome the effects of taxation, inflation and the various government pay restraint policies. Apart from this there is an element of the market place, each employer trying to attract staff with a better benefit package. The question of the utility of fringe benefits and their incentive effect is much more obscure. On the one hand they could be lumped together with financial reward and debated as part of the 'does money motivate' syndrome. Alternatively, some believe they fall on the 'statisfier' side of Herzberg's line in that they are a symbol of recognition of achievement and effort. It is fair to say that some fringe benefits have the effect of tying employees to an employer, eg low-interest mortgages, but it is also probably true that many employees identify more with fringe benefits than the impersonal pay slip, giving a positive effect on job satisfaction.

The expressions 'benefit package' and 'reward package' are now becoming part of the jargon of remuneration specialists. They signify a wider view of rewards, embracing both pay and the range of fringe benefits. We may even move towards the American concept of a 'cafeteria' system, whereby the member of staff chooses from a range of benefits on offer to an agreed value. It seems quite appropriate to treat employment rewards in a more comprehensive manner in view of the increasing range of fringe benefits.

Recommended reading

McBeath, G. and Rands, D. N., *Salary Administration*, 3rd ed., Business Books, 1976.

Lupton, T. and Bowey, A., *Wages and Salaries*, Penguin, 1974.

Lupton, T. and Gowler, D. *Selecting a Wage Payment System*, Kogan Page, 1970.

Whyte, W. F. *Money and Motivation*, Harper and Row, 1955.

Pratt, K. J. and Bennett, S. G., *Elements of Personnel Management*, Gee & Co. Ltd, 1979 (Chaps. 15–16).

11   Health and safety, welfare

Introduction

An examination of the development of personnel management reveals a continuing and underlying concern for the physical and mental welfare of employees. As will be discussed later, the nature of this concern and the facilities offered have changed radically over the past hundred years. In many respects the initiatives of individual employers have been usurped by statutory intervention, collective bargaining and the growth of the 'welfare state'. Nevertheless, expenditure on welfare provisions constitutes a large and growing element in many personnel budgets. Surveys have revealed that, as a proportion of payroll, average expenditure on welfare facilities has almost doubled since the war to around 30% in the USA and approximately 12% in the UK. A number of reasons have probably contributed to this trend, eg competition for skilled labour, a generally increased standard of living resulting in heightened worker expectations, high rates of direct taxation, particularly in middle and higher income brackets, government wage policies, etc.

An examination of the figures quoted above at first sight suggests a large discrepancy between average welfare expenditure in the UK and the USA. To some degree, of course, this is due to different levels of government-financed social service programmes. However it is also probably explained, at least in part, by the absence of any generally agreed definition of what is meant by 'welfare'. From the limited amount of recent literature on the subject a range of definitions and descriptions is apparent, some writers including and others excluding expenditure relating to legally required welfare provisions. Flippo, for example, lists three types of service:

1 *Economic* – providing economic security additional to basic pay and bonuses, including pensions, life insurance, etc.
2 *Recreational* – amusement and other social activities, such as dances and sports facilities.
3 *Facilitative* – cafeterias, legal and educational services, etc.

Hopkins, in *Industrial Welfare* (1955), suggests three alternatives: Economic, statutory and social.

The paucity of research into the area reveals equal confusion. Astall and Child in their study of 82 companies ('Employee Services', *Personnel Management*, Vol. 4, No. 8, 1972, pp. 539–541) list 13 categories, including typical welfare areas such as sports and social clubs, emergency loan arrangements, savings schemes, etc. However, also listed are areas more normally described as 'fringe benefits' or an ordinary part of the remunerative package, eg profit-sharing and sick pay. A similar story is told by a British Institute of Management survey published in April 1978. Here items such as time off in lieu of overtime and job-related training time are included. This diversity of views of welfare is perhaps best summarised by Hopkins who saw welfare as 'an attitude of mind on the part of management. . .'. Despite the absence of any precise definition, our own observations suggest that in practice there commonly exists an identifiable and discrete welfare function. It is important however that, for examination purposes, you are aware of this apparent 'grey area' and that you interpret and answer questions with this in mind.

Sample examination question

In what way does the law affect the working conditions of industrial employees? *(ACA)*

Key points

1 Inasmuch as a contract of employment exists, *all* working conditions are to some degree subject to the law. Statute also affects most aspects of employment, from recruitment to termination.

2 More specifically the Health and Safety at Work, etc. Act 1974 (HASAWA), superimposed over existing legislation, prescribes duties and standards.

3 An outline of the duties of employers, designers and suppliers of equipment and substances towards employees. The opportunities for participation through safety representatives and committees.

4 Means of enforcement: a unified inspectorate; improvement notices; prohibition notices; prosecution.

5 The relevance of other statutes. A summary of the Factories Act 1961.

Suggested answer

Inasmuch as a contract of employment exists between an employer and his employees, it may be argued that all working conditions are in some way affected by the law. In addition, there exists an array of legislation dealing with virtually all conditions of employment from the moment of recruitment until employment is terminated. More specifically however, the working conditions of industrial workers have been the subject of a whole series of statutes and other regulations. Indeed, so complex was the result that in 1974 a unifying act, the Health and Safety at Work, etc. Act (HASAWA), was introduced. The Act is an enabling measure superimposed over existing health and safety legislation. While much earlier law for the moment remains in force – particularly in this context, the Factories Act 1961 – it is intended that this shall gradually be repealed and replaced by revised regulations and codes of practice published under the umbrella of the HASAWA.

The Act covers all persons at work, whether employers, employees or the self-employed. Members of the general public are also protected in certain ways. Both general and specific duties are imposed on employers and employees, together with others engaged in the supply, design, etc. of articles used at work. So far as employers are concerned, the Act requires that they:

a Provide and maintain plant, systems and a work environment that, so far as is practicable, is safe and without risk to health;
b Make arrangements for the safe handling, storage, transport and use of articles and substances;
c Maintain the place of work in a safe and healthy state and with adequate and safe means of access and egress;
d Provide information, instruction, training and supervision necessary to ensure the health, safety and welfare of employees. Similar duties of care are imposed on designers, manufacturers, importers and suppliers of articles or substances used in the workplace.

An innovative measure under the Act was the formal recognition of the responsibility that individual workers have not only for their own safety, but also for others affected by their actions or omissions. Statutory duties of co-operation with management so far as health and safety matters are concerned were also imposed. In addition to such individual responsibilities the Act also provides the opportunity for collective participation in the promotion and development of health and safety measures through the appointment and establishment of safety representatives and committees. Appointed by independent trade unions and with terms of reference determined by a code of practice, representatives have the right not only to receive detailed information from management relevant to their duties, but also to take an active role in the investigation of accidents, potential hazards, the monitoring of health and safety standards, etc.

However laudable, statutory provisions are of little value unless capable of enforcement, and it is in this sense perhaps that the law may be seen most clearly to be affecting the working conditions of all persons at work, irrespective of status. Prior to 1974 the plethora of relevant statute was 'enforced' by a variety of specialist inspectors, each responsible for a specific aspect of industrial or commercial activity and often with very little 'muscle' so far as enforcement was concerned. Gathered together under the control of the Health and Safety Executive, the 1974 Act created a unified inspectorate with wide-ranging terms of reference and strengthened powers of enforcement. In particular, if an inspector is of the opinion that a person is contravening a relevant statutory provision, or has done so in circumstances which suggest that the contravention is likely to re-occur, he may issue an improvement notice. This requires that the contravention be remedied within a given period. In more serious instances a prohibition notice may be issued, directing that certain activities should not be carried on unless the matters specified in the notice are remedied. Should such notices be contravened, or indeed should some other statutory duty of regulation be breached, the Act provides for the person(s) responsible to be prosecuted. Currently the maximum penalty for such offences is an unlimited fine and/or imprisonment for up to two years. Annual reports published by the Health and Safety Executive reveal very clearly that such means of enforcement are readily and regularly used.

As mentioned earlier, for the moment other statute relating to the working conditions of industrial workers remains operative: in particular the Factories Act 1961. Like the 1974 Act, the 1961 Factories Act is a piece of consolidating legislation which lays down specific provisions regarding:

1 The cleaning and decoration of premises;
2 The working space allocated to each employee;
3 Heating, lighting and ventilation;
4 Lavatory and washing facilities;
5 First aid facilities;
6 The construction and maintenance of machinery, lifts, gangways, stairs, etc;
7 Fire precautions;
8 The employment of women and young persons.

Very similar provisions exist to protect workers in areas other than those designated under the 1961 Act, eg the Offices, Shops and Railway Premises Act 1963. Other statute and regulations exist which relate to the specific needs and problems of particular industries, eg the Agriculture (Safety, Health and Welfare Provisions) Act 1956, the Mineral Workings (Offshore Installations) Act 1971. In this way, irrespective of status, job, or the particular type of industry concerned, the law not only affects, but to an increasing degree prescribes and regulates the working conditions of industrial employees.

Further examination questions

1 What are the main provisions of the Health and Safety at Work, etc. Act 1974? *(ACA)*

2 Are the requirements of the 1974 Health and Safety at Work Act likely to have a major impact on company personnel activities in coming years? If so, in what main ways? *(ICSA)*

3 Discuss the arguments for and against the inclusion of safety within the personnel function. *(IPM)*

4 Discuss the scope of and justification for employee welfare services in present-day organisations. *(IPM)*

5 What cost-benefit calculations should a company make in deciding the range of employee services it should provide? (IPM)

6 How has the concept of employee welfare changed in recent years? *(ICSA)*

General comments on questions

Question 1 requires a straightforward outline of the main provisions of the 1974 HASAWA. This has already been discussed in the suggested answer above. A good answer would briefly explain the enabling nature of the Act and that it imposes duties on _all_ persons at work. A discussion of the means by which the Act is to be enforced would also be appropriate.

Question 2 while requiring some demonstration of knowledge of the 1974 Act, also seeks to discover your understanding of its day-to-day significance for employers. Irrespective of whether or not the Act may be considered an unqualified success, it is apparent that its influence has been widely felt by employers and employees alike. With increased awareness has come heightened expectation so far as health and safety standards are concerned. In general terms, the Act extends management responsibility to include _all_ aspects of health and safety in the workplace. For the first time there exists a statutory duty to formulate health and safety policies, and to establish structures for the implementation and control thereof. Considerable emphasis is placed on consultation; the Act, associated regulations and a code of practice require a very real partnership with employee representatives so far as health and safety matters are concerned. The apparent readiness of the Health and Safety Executive to use its enforcement powers likewise has both financial and practical significance for the day-to-day management of any function in any organisation, irrespective of its business. However, since in most organisations it is the personnel function which has particular responsibility for such matters, the Act's impact on the personnel management activities is clearly considerable. While for some time the function has exercised an advisory and liaison role so far as health and safety are concerned, the now more rigorous statutory requirements increasingly require that a monitoring role be adopted. It is often argued that rather than continuing in its traditionally advisory capacity, the personnel function becomes increasingly executive. Undoubtedly the HASAWA has reinforced this trend by imposing a policing role. For a more detailed examination of the consequences of such a shift in authority, you are referred to the suggested answer in Section 2 dealing with the personnel function and the role of the personnel manager.

Whether or not safety should continue to be a personnel responsibility is the substance of **Question 3**. While the question refers to safety, it is, in our opinion, artificial to separate this from industrial health matters. The reasons for the allocation of health and safety to the personnel function are largely historical, having to do with the function's welfare origins. Prior to the 1974 Act, it was a responsibility which many line managers were happy to leave in the hands of the personnel department. Thus there built up in those departments considerable health and safety expertise. It is only with the need for the executive powers demanded by the HASAWA that any serious debate regarding responsibility has arisen.

An analysis of modern safety and health management activities reveals good reasons why it should remain a personnel function. With the emphasis on prevention rather than cure, it is apparent that much useful data can be gained from desk research through analysis of employee personal and medical records. Such records are, of course, normally strictly confidential and in the care of the personnel department. Research has shown that accidents are often caused not by chance, nor by a series of physical factors, but by the psychological state of the individuals concerned. It has been similarly demonstrated that accidents may be reduced by safety education and training. The HASAWA requires active consultation with trade unions and their representatives. All are areas in which the personnel function ought to have some expertise. A rather more contentious issue has to do with the role of the personnel function as 'custodian of the corporate conscience'.

On the other hand, it is apparent that there are good reasons for at least some aspect of overall responsibility being attached either to the production function, where it exists, or to an autonomous health and safety 'audit' function. The complexity of technology daily renders more impossible the task of any 'non-technical' safety officer. In recent years, again spurred by the HASAWA, greater attention has been given to engineering for safety – safety measures being built in at the design stage or applied where subsequent hazards have been identified. Some would argue that safety officers employed within the production function, by virtue of their proximity to potential problems and their role within the production management team, are more likely to be effective in the immediate day to day elimination of hazards. A more basic argument suggests that it is line managers who can exercise the greatest influence over health and safety matters and thus it is they who should be responsible.

In the introduction to this section reference was made to the degree of overlap that exists between welfare provision and 'fringe benefits', which are normally considered a part of the remuneration package. This overlap is likely to be apparent to some degree in answers to **Question 4**. Empirically it is apparent that where a specific welfare function exists, its responsibilities commonly include such areas as:

1 Medical facilities	7 Long service awards
2 Staff canteens	8 Savings schemes
3 Sports and social clubs	9 Benevolent funds
4 Company housing	10 Purchase discount schemes
5 Assistance with education	11 Free/subsidised transport
6 Nurseries	12 Counselling – legal, financial, domestic, etc.

Why should such facilities be offered? Clearly none are absolutely essential to the achievement of corporate objectives; yet, as discussed in the introduction, they constitute a large and growing expenditure heading in the personnel budget. Employers' motives for such provision are varied and complex. In some organisations there still exists a highly paternalistic attitude towards the welfare of employees. In others, such facilities are seen not as paternalism, but as a demonstration of the acceptance of a social responsibility, ie the provision of a decent work environment. Such employers recognise and apparently accept that employees are not simply factors of production, but are human beings whose private lives both affect and are affected by their work. Their humanity entitles them to humane treatment. Other motives are less altruistic. Often the intention is to aid recruitment and the retention of staff. The provision of subsidised meals, medical facilities, health insurance, etc assists in the maintenance of a healthy, attendant and productive staff. Enhanced morale, increased company loyalty and an improved public relations image are all common objectives.

Whether or not such objectives are achieved is a matter for argument. Certainly there seems to exist little evidence to suggest that welfare benefits motivate workers to work harder. All employees normally have access to welfare facilities regardless of how hard they work. In the absence of a direct reward-effort relationship, benefits may well be taken for granted, frequently to the point of not being used at all. So far as aiding recruitment and reducing labour turnover are concerned, employers most generous in offering welfare packages are often those most generous so far as wages and other more fundamental conditions of employment are concerned. The contribution of welfare services in such instances seems likely to be marginal. Indeed Herzberg's work on job satisfaction suggests that 'job benefits' are perhaps the least important of all job variables in the view of most workers. In many respects, therefore, the provision of welfare benefits must be considered an act of faith.

If the above is the case, can a financial cost-benefit justification for such facilities be established? This is the problem set by **Question 5**. Clearly it is unwise to plan expenditure without at least some attempt to evaluate the degree of return likely to be enjoyed in consequence. So far as the cost element in the equation is concerned, this is normally readily apparent or reasonably capable of being forecast. It is the benefit aspect that presents difficulties for reasons outlined in the comments on the previous question. Nevertheless some attempt at measurement may be made. A reduction in labour turnover, general absenteeism, absenteeism due to sickness, labour relations difficulties, together with increased ease of recruitment are all claimed benefits and are all capable of expression in financial terms, even if a precise apportionment of the contribution made by welfare services vis-à-vis other factors is not possible. On a more general basis, certain principles may be established:

1 The facilities should satisfy a real rather than supposed need.
2 The benefit or service should be available more cheaply when purchased on a group basis than when purchased by individual employees.
3 The service should include as many employees as possible so as to minimise per capita cost and avoid the financing of minority interests.

Question 6 requires a discussion of the changing role of welfare provision. An examination of the development of what is now known as personnel management reveals its roots in the highly paternalistic attitudes of employers such as Boulton and Watt, Rowntree and Cadbury. Such tended to assume almost feudal responsibility and authority for not only the physical and social, but often also the moral welfare of their employees. Frequently based on a real sense of moral duty, such concern also probably contained at least an element of self-interest in the creation of a stable and loyal, some might say captive, workforce. Later developments in welfare provision, whatever the announced intention, may in many instances be recognised as attempts to limit unionisation.

Although it may be identified to at least some degree in the management practices of Eastern-based companies operating in the UK, this paternalistic concept of welfare is fast disappearing. While certain areas of traditional welfare provision remain unaffected, many have now been brought within statutory control, eg the HASAWA.

Former privileges have now become employee rights, eg provisions relating to redundancy, dismissal, pregnancy, etc. Other aspects, eg pensions, medical care, pay while sick, etc, while still areas in which many employers take an active interest, are provided by government for most if not all citizens. The spread of unionisation and growth of collective bargaining have similarly translated much discretionary welfare provision, eg paid holidays, into standardised terms and conditions of employment. In some respects the welfare function has thus been translated from that of the initiation of caring, but optional services, to that of imposed and specific duties. In this way the function has been both forced and freed to examine alternative welfare opportunities. As a result much current welfare activity focuses not on the blanket provision of welfare facilities which are believed to be worthwhile, but instead on the interactive nature of pressures to which the modern worker is subject both at and away from work. While evident in activities instantly recognisable as being in the traditional welfare vein, eg ergonomics and counselling, this change in emphasis is also manifest by a greater concern for employees' mental growth and satisfaction through opportunities for participation, greater emphasis on training and development, job design, etc. It is at this point that the traditional concept of the peripheral welfare function vanishes completely, being replaced instead by a function integrated with essential task-orientated activities both within the personnel function and elsewhere.

Recommended reading

Armstrong, M. and Arscott, P., *An Employer's Guide to Health and Safety Management*, Kogan Page, 1976.

Beaumont, P. B., *Safety Legislation: The Trade Union Response*, IPM, 1979.

Selwyn, N. M., *Law of Employment*, Butterworths, 1980.

Martin, A. O., *Welfare at Work*, Batsford, 1967.

Wade, M. (ed.), *Personnel Manager's Guide to Employee Benefits*, Business Publications, 1967.

Pratt, K. J. and Bennett, S. G., *Elements of Personnel Management*, Gee & Co. Ltd, 1979 (Chaps. 17–18).

12 Industrial relations

Introduction

The number of examination questions on 'industrial relations' is so large and the scope so wide that it is difficult to know where to begin. As with one or two other topics, we have decided to offer two suggested answers in addition to the general comments.

Industrial relations is included in the 'management' syllabus of most professional examinations, by whatever name called, as well as in the more specialised subjects. This, in itself, presents you with difficulties as you may meet only one question from an area which probably merits a separate exam paper and requires an appropriate amount of study. The subject of industrial relations is also continually changing, being affected by events and influenced by economics, politics and legislation. It is, therefore, essential to keep abreast of the industrial relations scene by reading appropriate newspapers and journals.

In order to get the problem into perspective, we list below some of the major aspects of industrial relations about which a well prepared candidate should have knowledge. It should be understood that no list of this type is exhaustive and can only indicate the *main* areas of study.

1 The British industrial relations 'system'.
2 Trade unions: structure; organisation; aims and objectives; activities.
3 Employers' associations.
4 The government: its role as employer and legislator; Government Agencies (ACAS, CAC etc).
5 Collective bargaining: machinery; levels; scope; the role of shop stewards; procedures.
6 Union recognition and union membership agreements ('closed shops').
7 Industrial action: strikes and other forms.

We hope the above will give an indication of the subject areas from which examination questions may be drawn. Personal experience and the topicality of some subjects may assist you, but it must be stressed that the popular press is no substitute for a sound and balanced view of the subject in question. There is, unfortunately, no substitute for well directed reading and hard work when it comes to a sound knowledge of industrial relations and the plethora of legislation which surrounds it.

We have decided to deal with questions on worker participation and industrial democracy in a separate section. This separation is purely to give sufficient attention to the large number of questions in this area and to avoid extending the length of this section further. We acknowledge that this decision is purely arbitrary and that the two subjects are closely inter-related.

Sample examination question (1)

Describe what is meant, in the context of Britain, by the term 'collective bargaining'. *(IPM)*

Key points

1 Definition of collective bargaining with examples of alternatives. Factors for success.

2 Subject-matter of collective bargaining and increasing scope.

3 Collective bargaining machinery and levels.

4 The Donovan analysis and recent trends.

Suggested answer

Collective bargaining is a method of determining the conditions of employment of a group of employees. The bargain is in the form of agreement reached between an employer or group of employers and the representatives of a group of workers, usually a trade union or staff association. S. & B. Webb saw collective bargaining as the collective alternative to an individual bargaining over the 'price' of his labour. However, Flanders disagreed with this collective market bargaining approach and preferred the terms 'joint determination' or 'joint regulation' which denote a process which has no equivalent at the individual level.

Collective bargaining has been a central feature of British industrial relations for many years. This system has been historically a 'voluntary' one based upon the integrity of the parties concerned and largely unfettered by government interference or litigation. In fact, state regulation of conditions of employment could be considered as a further alternative to collective bargaining. For collective bargaining to be successful in the British setting, certain prerequisites are necessary. Firstly, the parties must be sufficiently organised, eg possessing a reasonable level of representation, authority and control. Secondly, they must be willing to recognise each other and their agreements must be observed by those affected.

Collective bargaining activity can be broadly divided into two areas. The first is matters of procedure, which will deal with the conduct of the parties in the settlement of terms and conditions of employment, eg methods of dealing with negotiation, grievances, disputes, etc. The other main area in which agreements are made is concerned with substantive matters, eg wages, hours etc. These two areas are not always clear-cut or easily distinguishable in the British context but they provide an approach to the main characteristics of the 'rule-making process'.

The subject-matter of collective bargaining has increased in scope considerably over the years. This has extended from basic wages and hours of work to such things as training, work methods, discipline and promotion. In theory there is now no limit to the subjects of collective bargaining, despite attempts by management to preserve its prerogatives in some areas. It is fair to say that many of the matters dealt with are concerned with the 'management aspects' of employment. N. W. Chamberlain considers that collective bargaining can be looked at as a marketing process or as an institutional system but also as a functional system which provides for participation in the management process by the workforce. These three views of collective bargaining might be taken to represent an evolutionary process from what R. E. Walton and R. B. McKersie described as 'distributive bargaining' towards 'interpretive bargaining'.

Having considered the substance of collective bargaining, it might be appropriate to consider the parties involved and where the bargaining takes place. Collective bargaining 'machinery', as it is termed, can take various forms. At national level typical negotiating machinery would comprise an employers' association on one side and a federation or number of separate trade unions on the other. At company level a joint committee made up of members of management representing the employer with trade union officials and/or shop stewards for the workers is typical. At shop floor level negotiations will normally take place between the management and shop stewards with a minimum of formality.

Collective bargaining machinery reflects the various levels at which bargaining takes place. Generally speaking, these would be:

a Industry (national);
b Company;
c Plant;
d Sub-plant.

It should be remembered that negotiations may be taking place simultaneously at all these levels. Industry-wide bargaining is a well established part of the British system, although these negotiations are often restricted to minimum terms of employment nowadays as opposed to the all-embracing conditions of some years ago. The terms of the average worker are now greatly influenced by negotiations at plant and sub-plant level, often carried out by lay union officials on behalf of their constituents.

The Donovan Commission noted this 'workplace margin' and also highlighted the growth of the 'informal' (shopfloor level) system at the expense of the 'formal' (national level). It was the adequacy of the 'informal' system to cope with this increasing load with which Donovan was concerned. Amongst other things it was suggested that comprehensive company and plant level procedural agreements be established in order to regularise relationships and bargaining at this level.

Many organisations have accepted the Donovan analysis to some degree and have introduced more formality into plant-level bargaining. Many have also attempted to move away from the 'power struggle' approach to collective bargaining and towards what might be termed a 'problem-solving' approach as prescribed by Walton and McKersie. However, Eric Batstone has recently suggested that a combination of the increased formality of plant bargaining with increased shop steward status, together with a tendency towards centralized management decision-making, has tended to encourage conflict rather than ameliorate it.

Sample examination question (2)

Explain the reasons for the development of unions and staff associations in banking in recent years. *(IOB)*

Key points

1 Introduction – background to growth of 'white collar' trade unionism.

2 Suggested causes of the development of unions and staff association in banking.
   – Economic and technical factors
   – Growth of size of organisations
   – Trade union recruitment strategies
   – Employers' attitudes
   – Social and attitudinal change

3 Summary and conclusions – difficulties of accurate explanations for events – predictions of future trends.

Suggested answer

The majority of bank employees would be termed 'white collar' workers in industrial relations jargon, most of them being within the clerical, administrative, technical or managerial sectors of the workforce. The 'white collar' sector of trade unionism is undoubtedly providing any growth in overall union membership. This is partly due, of course, to the change in occupations brought about by changing technology and new industries, with a concomitant decline in older heavy industries. But this does not explain the reasons why trade unions have also made large inroads into areas such as banking which have not been traditionally associated with trade unionism.

Although firm evidence is difficult to find, economic factors have been suggested as one cause of the development. Traditionally, staff employed in organisations such as banks have enjoyed terms and conditions of employment, not to mention job security, considerably better than those of the average blue collar worker. Over the years, however, they have seen their differentials eroded due to what they perceive as the advantages of collective bargaining and union strength. The need to restore their position in the pay hierarchy, linked to possible fears of redundancy due to the threat of new technology, are considered to be partly responsible for the growth in union membership.

The growing size of organisations has also been cited as a contributing factor to union development and the main clearing banks would certainly be considered large by most standards. Apart from the threats caused by mergers and reorganisations during the growth period, the majority of large organisations become bureacratised and impersonal. The staff concerned are less likely to identify with management than the white-collar staff of smaller organisations and may consider that they have little chance of influencing their pay and working conditions on an individual basis. The standardisation of terms of employment lends itself to trade unionism and unions will concentrate their recruitment efforts upon larger establishments.

In recent years some trade unions have become involved in intensive recruitment drives and recognition struggles. Membership has increased rapidly in cases such as ASTMS through a combination of agressive marketing, public relations exercises and mergers with various staff associations. There is little doubt that these activities have exploited favourable conditions within the white collar areas.

The attitudes of employers within banking and other parts of the financial sector have also had their effect upon developments. In some cases employers have been willing to encourage staff associations in the hope of excluding independent trade unions. However, some of these have become financially independent of the employers and have gained Certificates of Independence and full negotiating recognition. Some employers have recognised the benefits of strong trade unions and staff associations for the purpose of negotiating acceptable procedures and conditions of service for all staff.

Although some employers have been able to avoid trade unionism through a paternalistic approach to their staff, there is evidence that many staff wish to have more influence over their terms and conditions of employment. These aspirations can probably be linked to the feelings of vulnerability and 'missing out' referred to above. The large banks have, of necessity, recruited from a much wider social spectrum than previously and many employees come from a background in which trade unionism is not unfamiliar or decried.

Probably as a result of a combination of the factors referred to above, most of the large banks now recognise trade unions or staff associations to a greater or lesser extent. The developmental process has been long and complex and it is difficult to be precise when offering explanations for these developments. If economic and social trends continue, the growth of formal representation of clerical, administrative and managerial staff will persist in banking as well as many other sectors of industry.

Further examination questions

1 Conflict within an organisation may be regarded as avoidable or inherent, functional or dysfunctional. What are your views on conflict and what would be the implications of those views for management policies? *(IAM)*

2 How would you define good industrial relations and how would you measure progress towards improved industrial relations? *(ICSA)*

3 Why do some industries seem to be more strike-prone than others?
(*ICSA*)

4 If, as happens every day, a Martian landed in your front garden, and asked you: 'What is a procedural agreement?', what answer would you give to him/her/it? (*IPM*)

5 Assuming the existence of a Staff Association in a Building Society, draft that section of the Procedure Agreement designed for settling disputes. (*CBSI*)

6 How can membership of a staff association or trade union help an employee? Are there any disadvantages in membership? (*IOB*)

7 Discuss the arguments for and against legal powers being available to enable the enforcement of the 'closed shop'. (*ACA*)

8 What facilities are offered by the Advisory, Conciliation and Arbitration Service to the parties to help them resolve collective industrial disputes? (*IPM*)

9 To what extent do you consider the role and function of the Personnel Manager are being taken over by Staff Representative Bodies? (*CBSI*)

General comments on questions

Question 1 may not be recognised immediately as an 'industrial relations' question but we consider it sufficiently relevant to include it in this section. You will need to have a knowledge of the arguments put forward by such people as Alan Fox and his 'unitary' and 'pluralistic' views of organisations. Despite the exhortation of many managers to 'pull together' (a 'unitary' view), Fox maintains that commercial organisations are, in fact, 'pluralistic'. There is an inherent conflict of interests between management and the workers which must be recognised as a pre-requisite for any successful management policy. Having given your views on the nature of conflict in organisations (or the lack of it), you will be required to discuss its effects upon such things as industrial relations and advise on management policies to deal with the situation. There are also obvious implications for such things as industrial democracy and collective bargaining as well as overall management style.

Question 2 also requires a view to be taken of an organisation with regard to such things as conflict. If one adopted a 'pluralistic' approach, it might be appropriate to discuss the ways in which conflict is controlled and managed in order to create a 'healthy' environment. Indications of good industrial relations might be such things as the development of appropriate procedures, the degree of consultation and participation, labour turnover, absenteeism, the strike record etc. These should, however, only be treated as indicators and not as conclusive evidence. A low strike incidence may mask other forms of industrial action or unrest.

The subject of strike-proneness is also raised in **Question 3**. Despite the various theories which have been propounded over the years, there are very few conclusive answers to this question, particularly when making comparisons at an international level. There is also an implicit additional dimension to the question. This concerns the doubt surrounding the statistics upon which strike-incidence is based. Government statistics are based upon voluntary returns from industry and even then do not include many smaller strikes. This could imply that the industries which file returns most conscientiously could seem to be more strike prone! It is generally considered that nationalised industries are better at filing returns than those in the private sector although there is no firm evidence of this.

Given the dubious premise upon which the assumptions are based, there are various reasons that may be put forward. These include methods of production, geographical isolation, human relations, agitators, size of work groups etc. We do not have space to expand upon these theories here but several texts expand upon the arguments put forward and also point out the inevitable exceptions to the rule, eg R. Hyman (see recommended reading).

Questions 4 and 5 are both concerned with procedural agreements, the former being a general question and the latter requiring a more detailed treatment of a particular type of procedure.

Question 4 provides an opportunity to deal with the fundamentals of procedural agreements on the assumption that the reader has no prior knowledge of these or of industrial relations generally. This amount of scope can lull one into a false sense of security and lead to sloppy thinking, however. It is essential to ensure that you cover all aspects of the subject in a clear and concise manner. A good answer should at least cover the following:

a The industrial relations context in which procedural agreements are made.
b Definition and functions of procedural agreements, contrasted with agreements on substantive issues.
c Discussion of practical application of agreements and relevance to various situations; the Donovan analysis and subsequent developments.
d Examples of different types of procedural agreement and the stages of a typical procedure.
e Procedural inadequacy; the criteria for a sound procedure and the need for adaptation and change.

As with many general questions, it is important to ensure that you cover all aspects in a direct and economic style rather than becoming bogged down in a detailed treatment of just one or two areas.

Question 5 requires exactly the opposite approach to Question 4. Here the discipline is to concentrate on one specific task. No marks will be awarded for general discussions of procedural agreements. Although the question refers to a Staff Association and a Building Society, the agreement should not differ much from any other disputes procedure in principle. These usually follow an 'escalator' basis, with the number of stages and parties involved varying according to the type of organisation and its industrial relations structure. A typical outline might be:

Stage 1 Member of staff takes grievance to his supervisor. If no satisfaction –
Stage 2 Staff Association representative informed and both take up problem with supervisor. If no satisfaction within (defined number of) days –
Stage 3 Staff representative takes grievance to Senior Manager. If no satis-

faction within (defined number of) days (matter may now convert from a 'grievance' to a 'dispute') –

Stage 4 Matter discussed by joint committee of Staff Association and management. If problem not resolved –

Stage 5 Matter referred to arbitration panel or individual arbitrator as previously agreed.

It should be noted that grievance and disputes procedures are usually parts of the same process. A 'grievance' will become a 'dispute' once supported by the union or staff association and the case registered as a 'failure to agree'.

Question 6 might be seen as a different approach to Sample Examination Question (2), which deals with the reasons for the development of representative bodies in banking in recent years. It is a classic 'advantages/disadvantages' type of question but requires more than a peremptory treatment. It is advisable to take a detached view with this type of question, as one man's 'help' might be another man's 'interference'. From this viewpoint, the following could be mentioned and enlarged upon:-

Help

1 Strength of representation on terms of employment.
2 Protection against discrimination, redundancy etc.
3 Possible financial benefits over and above those provided by employer.
4 Greater knowledge of management policies etc.

Disadvantages

1 Deprivation of individual bargaining rights.
2 Lack of personal contact and communication.
3 Less recognition of individual merit.

Question 7 deals with the perennial subject of the 'closed shop', but from a particular angle. Although we have included only one sample question on this topic, we could have given several other examples which are either directly or indirectly concerned with this area. It goes without saying, therefore, that your knowledge of this subject must extend beyond that given in the popular press if you are to tackle industrial relations questions successfully.

Closed shops, or 'union membership agreements' as the law refers to them, produce a great deal of emotion among commentators and critics. It is fatal for candidates to fall into the trap of discussing closed shops in this way. As with any examination question, a balanced and informed account is required.

The question is presumably referring to the statutory position on trade union membership and the dismissal implications. Subsequent to the Trade Union and Labour Relations Acts of 1974 and 1976, dismissal was considered 'fair' if there was a union membership agreement and an employee refused to become or remain a member of the specified union(s), unless the employee objected on grounds of religious belief to being a member of any trade union. This position has now been modified by the Employment Act 1980, whereby an employee who objects 'on grounds of conscience or other deeply held personal convictions' can opt out of present or future closed shop agreements.

Apart from the political and ethical arguments for compelling an individual to join a trade union or not, there are the more basic arguments of allowing 'free riders' to obtain the benefits gained by the unions without paying subscriptions. Some managers may also argue that, at the pragmatic level, they would prefer a

100% membership situation. Surveys have shown that better industrial relations and a calmer environment are amongst the benefits to be gained from a closed shop situation.

Whether or not the law should be used to control the situation is an argument which has received a great deal of publicity in recent times and will no doubt continue into the future. Current newspaper reports and articles will provide the topical detail required.

Question 8 is relatively straightforward in that it requires a factual account of facilities offered by ACAS. The question is, however, slanted towards help with collective industrial disputes. The traditional activities of conciliation, mediation and arbitration have been continued by ACAS with the assistance of the Central Arbitration Committee (CAC) and these activities form the core of the range of assistance available. Several booklets are issued by ACAS which outline its activities and these are often available from local Department of Employment offices. The Annual Reports of ACAS provide further details, and specific examples of the work of the service are often reported in the press and various journals.

Question 9 might present difficulties on two counts. Firstly, there is the temptation to write all you know about the role of the personnel manager. Secondly, the concept of his role being 'taken over' may in itself be difficult to grasp. We assume that the examiner is referring to the fact that trade unions and staff associations are becoming increasingly involved in areas of pay, discipline, health and safety, redundancy etc through collective bargaining and consultative machinery as well as at the personal representation level. There is also a sense in which they both act as a management 'watchdog' with regard to statutory requirements and the rights of the workforce.

You are presumably required to discuss the traditional personnel management activities and the ways in which the activities of staff representative bodies overlap with these. Despite the growth of activities by these bodies in what we traditionally considered 'management' areas, we do not consider that the personnel manager's role is being 'taken over'. Rather his methods of communication may have altered and he will increasingly need to develop policies and procedures in consultation with staff representatives. Despite this change at the 'tactical' level, his management role would appear to be largely unchanged in principle if one assumes a 'pluralistic' view of organisations.

Recommended reading

Clegg, H. A., *The System of Industrial Relations in Great Britain*, Blackwell, 1976.
Anthony, P. D., *The Conduct of Industrial Relations*, IPM, 1977.
Flanders, A. (ed.), *Collective Bargaining*, Penguin, 1969.
Daniel, W. W., *Beyond the Wage-Work Bargain*, PEP, 1970.
Hyman, R., *Strikes*, Fontana, 1972.
Pratt, K. J. and Bennett, S. G., *Elements of Personnel Management*, Gee & Co. Ltd, 1979 (Chaps. 19–23).

13 Industrial democracy and participation

Introduction

The term 'industrial democracy' has become part of the language in this country over the past ten years or so. It has been thrust to the forefront of discussion due to various influences and pressures. Some of these pressures have emanated from institutions such as the EEC, the TUC and various government agencies. Other moral, sociological and psychological influences have been less easily identifiable. But what is 'industrial democracy'? This question is difficult to answer in precise terms, but if equated with civil democracy it could be termed the right of individuals and groups to be consulted, informed and involved in matters concerning their working lives. In practical terms it implies greater participation by the workforce in decisions affecting their livelihood. How, then, can this participation be implemented?

Examination questions on worker participation in decision-making tend to prompt essays about 'workers on the board'. This is probably attributable to the influence of the debate which has been continuing for some years in this country, due in large measure to our obligations under the EEC Fifth Directive. This is concerned with the harmonisation of Company Law within member states and includes proposals for implementing a system of worker-directors on the boards of certain private sector companies. Our response, or lack of response to this directive is partly history and can be studied elsewhere by those who are unfamiliar with events. (This subject will be enlarged upon in the course of the questions dealt with below).

To equate industrial democracy with representation at board level would, in our view, be failing to appreciate the much wider scope of the subject. A comprehensive treatment of the subject would include such areas as:

Collective bargaining
Joint consultation
Pay systems
Job design
Co-ownership
Communication systems
Management style
Motivation
Worker directors

The above random list hopefully indicates that the subject embraces many areas of general concern to management apart from board representation. Many would consider that there are, in fact, many more practical ways of increasing worker participation than to provide places on the board for worker representatives.

This wide scope may not be of particular encouragement to those embarking upon examinations. How should you marshall the facts and bring some logic to this seemingly complex subject? We personally find that K. F. Walker's 'four forms of democratisation' provide a useful frame-work for general questions on this subject. For those unfamiliar with these we strongly recommend his book (see reading list). For a brief reference, see the suggested answer to the sample examination question below.

In order to answer examination questions successfully on this subject you will require both factual knowledge and the ability to put forward current arguments. Some of these arguments will be developed in this section but we would again recommend that you take an interest in current reports and articles. Even as we write, a new EEC draft Directive has been issued with proposals on procedures for informing and consulting the employees of undertakings with a 'complex structure' on a wide range of matters. This could, in fact, cover any company with two or more units of more than 100 employees and includes the transmission of information to employee representatives *before* certain 'sensitive' decisions are made in order to allow for consultation. Although this draft Directive has already met with opposition in the UK, it is typical of the level of activity in this field.

Sample examination question

> What are the arguments for employee participation in management decisions? How can such an aim be implemented? (*ICSA*)

Key points

1 Generally accepted arguments in favour of greater participation with note of dissentients.

2 Types of democratisation – Walker's analysis.

3 More detailed discussion of different approaches and implications of implementation.

4 Conclusions on practicalities of different schemes.

Suggested answer

The arguments for employee participation in management decisions will depend upon the parties putting forward the arguments. However, the proponents of increased participation might put forward the following advantages:

a A means of extending democracy from the civil and political spheres to the workplace.

b A method of increasing the satisfaction and personal development of people at work.
c A means of improving industrial relations.
d A way of increasing the efficiency of organisations.

From these arguments it is apparent that, potentially, there appear to be benefits for the workforce and the organisation. These arguments are not, however, irrefutable and many on the management side would argue that managerial decisions are best made by those with the responsibility and expertise to make them. It is also fair to state that many workers are not particularly interested in participating in management decisions. Even so, there is a generally acknowledged and growing body of opinion which supports the arguments in favour of increased participation. Apart from the social pressures for change, bodies such as the EEC are attempting to influence a more democratic climate within organisations.

If the general arguments for increased participation are accepted, how might this arise and how can it be put into practice? K. F. Walker's 'four forms of democratisation' may be a useful starting point. He considers that participation can take place in four main ways.

1 Through sharing *ownership* of the enterprise, eg share issues.
2 By giving employees greater say in their *terms and conditions of employment* through, for instance, collective bargaining of greater scope.
3 By allowing employees to participate in the *government* of the enterprise at board level.
4 Through greater participation in the *management process* of the organisation through various, often informal means.

The ways in which these areas could be 'democratised' have been briefly referred to under Walker's analysis. However, these may be clarified by giving some examples and amplification.

Some would suggest that true participation cannot take place without the rewards and responsibilities of ownership. The John Lewis Partnership and the Scott Bader Commonwealth are examples of a fairly radical approach to employee ownership, but many organisations have introduced various share ownership schemes in recent years. Ownership of the enterprise strikes at the heart of our economic and social systems and, although isolated cases claim success, there are obvious problems of pursuing this course to any depth.

Terms of employment have been subject to negotiation for many years in a great number of organisations. Many consider, however, that there is still tremendous scope for increased participation in this area. The development of collective bargaining over the years has already provided a much wider agenda than the 'pay, hours and holidays' of years ago. However, many consider the transition from 'distributive' to 'integrative' bargaining as described by Walton and McKersie is the most fruitful and practical means of increasing worker participation.

Participation at board level has been the subject of a great deal of debate and activity over the past decade. As a member of the EEC, Britain is subject to the Fifth Directive which requires that attempts be made to find acceptable methods of introducing worker-directors to larger organisations. Experiments have been attempted in the nationalised sector but there have been practical problems. Although lip service is paid to this indirect form of participation, ie through representatives, there does not appear to be much interest at grass-roots level.

The forms of participation mentioned above tend to be 'indirect', that is through representative bodies in which the individual worker has no direct involvement. Walker's fourth type of democratisation deals with a more 'direct' approach through participation in the management precess. This may take many forms from improved communications through job redesign to new reward systems. It may involve formal and informal work groups but will almost certainly require a change in management style. Much research has been carried out in these areas and successful schemes such as those at Volvo, Saab and ICI have been widely reported. The more successful schemes of worker participation appear to incorporate a wide consultative process at the planning stage. It is quite possible that a high level of consultation and communication is all that most workers require.

Assuming the pressures for increased democracy and participation in managerial decisions do not abate, how might these ideals be implemented? The above discussion has, hopefully, highlighted the main areas of activity to date but which should management choose? There is no simple answer to this and the response will no doubt vary from one organisation to another. It is likely that progress will need to be made on several fronts. There is little doubt that those who do not adopt some of the techniques for greater 'direct' participation may find the 'indirect' pressures taking the initiative from them.

Further Examination questions

1 In the present trend towards employee participation, how can a manager fulfil his responsibilities and still retain his authority?

(IAM)

2 What are the main advantages/difficulties of involving employees in the decision making process? *(IAM)*

3 Much has been written in recent years on the subject of 'employee participation' or 'industrial democracy'. Define clearly your understanding of this and detail the part which the personnel department must play in developing effective systems of participation. *(CBSI)*

4 What are the arguments for and against the extension of industrial democracy through the appointment of employee representatives to company boards? *(ICSA)*

5 How will the extension of 'worker participation' schemes affect the distinction traditionally drawn between negotiation and consultation? *(IPM)*

6 There is currently a good deal of discussion of the desirability of increasing worker or trade union participation in industrial decision-making. To what extent are 'trade union purposes' likely to

be served by the legislative creation of supervisory (or two-tier) boards as devices for increasing such 'participation'? *(IPM)*

7 Discuss the possible meanings of the term 'participation' when used in an industrial/commercial context. How far do you believe that 'participation' holds any promise of improving industrial relations? *(ICSA)*

General comments on questions

Question 1 poses the classic dilemma of increasing employee participation and raises many of the practical problems involved. Mick Marchingtron's article in *Personnel Management* for April 1981 highlights the different perspectives taken by management and trade union representatives. This conflict of interests has been clearly identified by Fox and subsequent discussion on the 'pluralistic' view of organisations. The question might also embrace the subject of management style by comparing the 'Theory X' approach with the 'Theory Y' in McGregor's terms. Theory Y assumptions about the average worker – that he possesses motivation, imagination and commitment, given the right conditions and leadership – need not imply any loss of authority by the manager. The differences between 'position power' and actual authority would also be relevant to a discussion of this type.

We see this question as a broad discussion of the ways in which the aspirations of the workforce and management objectives can be accommodated through a variety of channels and techniques. Many of these have been mentioned in the introduction to this section and the suggested answer above.

Question 2 would also embrace many of the arguments used in the suggested answer. The possible advantages might include increased motivation and/or job satisfaction, together with subsequent increases in efficiency and productivity as well as improved industrial relations. The most likely areas of success are those which involve advantages for workers *and* management. The difficulties could be divided into attitudinal problems and the practical problems of implementing ideas. Intransigent attitudes are a fundamental problem for any change in policy and must be recognised before any scheme is attempted. Problems of implementation are, therefore, closely linked to the psychological climate but might also include technical and financial constraints upon changes in structure or process. The difficulties of changing to a 'Volvo' style of production for a company such as Ford would be an example of the practical aspects.

Question 3 also covers some of the ground of the previous two questions and is not too dissimilar from the sample examination question above. You would do well to use Walker's categorisation of the main areas of 'democratisation' again in this situation. From this starting-point it would be relatively straightforward to discuss the role of the personnel department, particularly in the areas of job design, consultation and collective bargaining.

Unlike the more general questions above, **Question 4** concentrates on industrial democracy through the appointment of worker-directors. The arguments for and against their appointment can be made at an emotional, political or practical level and will need to be ascribed to the parties involved. The arguments have been well aired in various reports such as Bullock and some of those put forward by the trade union movement are outlined below.

For	*Against*
1 Dilutes 'management prerogative'	1 Forces trade unions to promote aims contrary to their beliefs
2 Increases company's accountability to workers	2 Trade unions would become jointly responsible for management decisions
3 Provides greater access to information	3 Confuses issues and weakens trade union independence
4 Allows trade unions to initiate and influence decisions at high level	4 Weakens trade unions' ability to oppose management decisions through collective bargaining
5 Extends collective bargaining to the board room	

It would also be useful to mention the practical difficulties which have been experienced in the experiments at British Steel and the Post Office. Peter Shaw was a trade union representative on the main board of the Post Office for two years from 1978 to 1980. His article in *Personnel Management* (August 1980) defines some basic criteria for the successful introduction of worker-directors. Firstly, he considers that both management and unions must have a positive philosophy on participation. Negative attitudes on either side would stifle any potential for development. Trust is stated as another essential. Resentment and suspicion will not encourage an open and constructive climate. Time, patience and a willingness to innovate are suggested by Shaw as further ingredients for success. Role conflict has also been cited by worker-directors involved in these schemes; they are accepted neither by their fellow directors nor by their former colleagues on the shop floor. Practical examples like the above add a further dimension to the wider arguments for and against employee representatives on company boards and will provide a more interesting and comprehensive answer to this type of question.

Questions 5, 6 and 7 all refer to the industrial relations aspects of industrial democracy.

Question 5 requires a discussion of negotiation and consultation and the ways in which the traditional content of each might be affected by participation schemes. The examiner is presumably alluding to the possible 'merger' of items on the agendas of both these activities through greater recognition of the workers' right to be involved in a wider range of decisions.

It should be recognised that many items have indeed been transferred from consultation to negotiation over the years. Whether or not the scope of collective bargaining has widened with or without the willing consent of management is difficult to state in general terms. The extent of this development in any particular organisation will presumably have a bearing upon the degree to which 'worker participation schemes' will affect the situation. If these 'schemes' included real machinery for increasing the workers' ability to influence a wide range of decisions, then the answer to the question might be 'a great deal'. On the other hand, if the schemes tended to be more concerned with individual involvement in work design and on the job decisions, the traditional subject-matter of consultation and negotiation may be less directly affected.

Question 6, like Question 4, concentrates upon the 'workers on the board' aspect of participation but refers specifically to the two-tier system used in Germany and Holland.

An obvious starting point is to define what is meant by 'trade union purposes'. This expression appears to be an amalgam of both the objectives of trade unions and the methods employed to achieve them. Although both these elements will vary in detail from one union to another, it is probably safe to employ some generalisations. The objectives listed by the TUC in its evidence to the Donovan Commission serve as a good guide; in summary these amount to improving the working lives of their members, the central and traditional objective of trade unionism.

Many within the trade union movement would argue that if workers are to further their interests, they need to be involved in major policy decisions which affect their livelihood. Others argue that worker representation at board level is not the best way of achieving this. The arguments put forward for and against worker representation at board level have been discussed above under Question 4. The single-tier versus two-tier arguments have also been well argued and the 1978 White Paper suggested a two-tier system despite the Bullock majority report favouring a single-tier board. The trade union movement appears undecided upon which system it prefers, leaving aside the arguments for and against *any* form of board representation. The arguments for representation on a supervisory board under a two-tier system revolve around fears of loss of identity. It is argued that if workers serve on a supervisory board, it is clearly separated from management and can exercise any powers 'independently'. Against this, of course, it will be pointed out that unless they participate in a management board, decisions will only come to the notice of worker-representatives after they have been taken and the ability to influence events will be greatly diminished.

Question 7 is partially covered by previous discussion and it also emphasises the industrial relations aspects of increased participation. After a discussion of various types of participation it will be necessary to enter into a realistic appraisal of the effects of these upon the industrial relations climate within an industrial/commercial organisation. Fox's 'unitary/pluralistic' syndrome is again relevant to this discussion and a balanced view is essential. Many practical schemes have demonstrated that greater participation can create better industrial relations, but correlations are often clouded by other factors. All new schemes bring difficulties as well as advantages. The long debate on board-level participation referred to above is one example of this type of problem. The causes of poor industrial relations are themselves often extremely complex and to ascribe any improvement to a particular principle such as participation is to oversimplify the situation.

Recommended reading

Walker, K. F., *Industrial Democracy*, Times Publication Department, 1970.
BBC, *Democracy at Work*, BBC Trade Union Studies, 1977.
Wallace Bell, D., *Industrial Participation*, Pitman, 1979.
Pratt, K. J. and Bennett, S. G., *Elements of Personnel Management*, Gee &
    Co Ltd, 1979 (Chap. 21).

14 Dismissal

Introduction

Before the Contracts of Employment Act 1963, employees had no right to notice of dismissal unless specifically dealt with in a contract of employment or some other provision. Even after 1963, when most employees were granted some degree of statutory protection, a dismissed employee had no right of action unless he could show that agreed or sufficient notice had not been given, or that there had been some other breach of contract. In such instances redress for wrongful dismissal was available via the Courts. Such a right still exists today.

Nevertheless, so long as an employer gave the correct period of notice there was little any employee could do, however unfair he felt the reason for his dismissal to be. Such a situation encouraged less conscientious employers to adopt a cavalier approach to their dealings with staff, hiring and firing with little regard for the social or psychological consequences of their action.

In the Industrial Relations Act 1971, employees were protected against such arbitrary treatment for the first time. Under this Act, an employee who felt himself *unfairly* dismissed, ie dismissed for no apparent good reason, was granted a right of appeal to an industrial tribunal. If, after hearing the case, the tribunal found a dismissal unfair, it had power to award compensation or recommend reinstatement. Such original provisions still remain essentially intact, though much modified in detail by subsequent amendments. The nature of the current arrangements will be dealt with below.

Largely because of its highly emotive nature, dismissal is a subject regularly reviewed by politicians. It is important therefore that you ensure that you are up to date so far as regulations and procedures are concerned. Outline reports of changes are normally to be found in the national press. However, more detailed summaries are usually contained in specialist journals such as *Personnel Management* and *The Department of Employment Gazette*. Guides to current regulations are also available, usually free, from government employment offices.

Sample examination question

> What kind of policy and procedures would you advise for an organisation, so that it could minimise the risk of problems of any kind arising from allegedly 'unfair' dismissals? (*ICSA*)

Key points

  1 Brief explanation of 'unfair dismissal' and the possible consequences.

  2 While not law, adherance to the provisions of the ACAS Code of Practice No. 1 will provide a sound basis for company policy and procedures and evidence of reasonable behaviour should a claim be made.

  3 The joint formulation and publication of disciplinary rules and procedures.

  4 Recommended essential characteristics of any disciplinary procedure.

  5 An outline disciplinary/dismissal procedure.

Suggested answer

The Industrial Relations Act 1971 provided for the first time that an employee who felt himself unfairly dismissed should have the right of access to an Industrial Tribunal, which after hearing the facts of the case should have the power to award compensation or recommend reinstatement. This provision has been modified in various ways: in some ways extended, in others restricted. For an employer the consequences of having to face a claim for unfair dismissal are potentially expensive in terms of management time, legal costs and compensation, not to mention the possibility of industrial relations difficulties. It is therefore essential that organisations are not only aware of the pitfalls but also actively seek to avoid them. Clearly the best way of achieving such an objective is by the development of carefully considered and well publicised policies and procedures.

In formulating such arrangements a useful starting point is to consider the ACAS Code of Practice No 1 on disciplinary procedures. While the Code is not legally binding, an employer who can show that he has adhered to its provisions both in the preparation and operation of disciplinary procedures will have a significant advantage in demonstrating the reasonableness of his behaviour if required to do so by a tribunal. Particular emphasis is placed by the Code on the need for the adequate publication of rules of conduct and the procedures likely to be adopted should they be breached. It is recommended that wherever possible employees and their representatives should participate in the preparation of procedures and policies. Clearly this is advantageous as a means of reducing the possibility of industrial relations difficulties resulting from disciplinary proceedings, since a procedure mutually prepared and acknowledged stands more chance of acceptance than one unilaterally imposed by management.

The Code also recommends certain characteristics essential to any satisfactory disciplinary procedure. A clear statement should exist regarding different levels of management and their degree of authority so far as disciplinary action is concerned. In any case, the Code recommends that a supervisor should not have the authority to dismiss an immediate subordinate. Considerable emphasis is placed on the need for justice not only to be done, but to be seen to be done. Thus employees should in all cases be given the chance not only to state their case, but to do so accompanied by a friend or representative. A right of appeal should exist in all cases with provision for independent arbitration if the parties to the procedure so wish it.

Except in cases of gross misconduct, no employee should be dismissed for a first offence. Whether a first offence or not, no disciplinary action should be taken until the matter has been thoroughly investigated. Any action subsequently taken should always be explained together with details of any appeals procedure. Records of employee warnings should be reviewed regularly and, depending on the nature of the offence, details should be struck from the record after a fixed period.

Other guidelines have emerged from tribunal decisions. Thus it appears that whatever the adopted rules, a fresh procedure should apply in each case of complaint against the employee, ie a first warning for one offence should not be followed by a second warning for another. Procedures once established should normally be followed through before dismissal is instituted; and indeed whatever penalty is imposed, it must be consistent and not too severe when compared with previous cases within the organisation. Such are generalisations. What might be the pattern of a typical procedure?

Though at first sight a little long-winded, it would appear that in order to protect itself from claims, an organisation would do well to consider the adoption of a scheme such as that outlined below:

1 When an offence first occurs, a warning by the immediate superior is all that is normally required.
2 If the offence' re-occurs, the immediate superior should again warn the employee concerned, recording only the briefest details. The offender should also be advised of action to be taken should the offence occur again and of any right of appeal. At such an interview the opportunity to be accompanied by a friend or representative should be given. Only in extreme cases should a written warning be given at this stage. In any case, details of both oral and any written warnings should be removed from the employee's file after a given period.
3 Should the offence be committed yet again, a formal interview normally conducted by a senior member of management together with the immediate superior will normally follow. The employee should again, if he chooses, be accompanied by either a friend or a representative. A final warning should be issued and confirmed in writing together with details of the possible consequences of a further offence and any right of appeal. Arrangements should be made for the warning to be removed from the employee's file after a given period.
4 If a further offence does indeed occur, a further formal interview as in 3 above will normally take place, followed by appropriate disciplinary action. Again all details should be confirmed in writing. It is important that whatever action is taken it should be seen to be appropriate bearing in mind the nature of the offence, the employee's record, and the way in which similar offences

have been previously treated.

5 Following disciplinary action, or at any other stage in the procedure, a right of appeal should exist. To whom such an appeal is made will vary from organisation to organisation. Typically, it will be to a member of senior management, a joint disciplinary committee or to an external arbitrator.

Such a procedure, while affording considerable protection against claims, cannot of course be guaranteed totally watertight. Even the most thorough and reasonable of procedures can never support a wholly unfair reason for dismissal. Similarly, there will be instances where even the application of an agreed procedure such as that above will still result in industrial action being taken by colleagues of an aggrieved employee. All that can be done to minimise such problems is, as outlined above, to involve employees and their representatives both in the preparation of the procedure and at all stages in its operation. It should be noted that for smaller organisations the Employment Act 1980 does provide some relief, in as much as it requires tribunals to consider the size and administrative resources of the employer's undertaking when considering the reasonableness of action taken. It is, however, too early to determine to what extent this will permit such employers to ignore previously stated guidelines.

Further examination questions

1 What should be the guiding principles for a company's disciplinary procedure? *(ICSA)*

2 Write a guide, as if addressed to a newly promoted manager, on all relevant aspects of the conduct of a disciplinary interview.

(ICSA)

3 It is a commonly held view that the legislation relating to unfair dismissal has seriously eroded the powers of employers.
   a Outline the law relating to unfair dismissal; and
   b argue the case for and against this view. *(CBSI)*

4 Consider the view that the employee now enjoys too much legal protection in respect of dismissals. *(IPM)*

General comments on questions

Question 1 requires the same treatment as the sample examination question.

   Question 2 needs a rather different approach. What is required is a practical working guide to the business of conducting a disciplinary interview. Clearly, in order to avoid the possibility of an unfair dismissal claim occurring, it would be as well in such a case to make the newly appointed manager aware of the current legal situation and the possible consequences for the employer should a successful claim occur. A description of the organisation's agreed disciplinary procedure would also be appropriate, identifying very clearly the manager's role, authority and *limits to his authority*. In many ways, therefore, the answer will share many of the elements of the suggested answer. In addition, what is required, in our opinion, is advice on the manager's attitude should formal disciplinary action become necessary. Such guidelines would probably recommend that:

1 Whether taking formal or informal disciplinary action, a judicial attitude should be preserved at all costs.
2 Disciplinary action should *always* be taken in private.
3 An attempt should be made to produce some positive result from the most negative of disciplinary situations.
4 Discipline should be prompt and consistent: favouritism, however natural, should not be evident in such proceedings.
5 After the disciplinary action, the supervisor should attempt to restore normality as quickly as possible in his dealings with staff concerned.

As indicated, **Question 3** requires an outline of the law relating to unfair dismissal followed by a discussion of the extent to which employees today enjoy too much protection. The latter is also the substance of **Question 4**. In answering such questions it is clearly possible to approach the problem at a number of levels from the wholly emotional to the strictly legal and from a variety of intransigent political viewpoints. However, dogma of any kind is almost certainly what the examiner does not want. A balanced answer is required, presenting the evidence on both sides.

As discussed in the introduction, employees today certainly enjoy significantly more protection against dismissal than twenty years ago. The consequences for an employer who unfairly dismisses an employee are potentially severe. However, the situation must be seen in perspective. Just as an employer has a right to be able to terminate the employment of an unsatisfactory employee, so too, one would argue, an employee has a right not to have his livelihood terminated simply on the whim or fancy of his employer. There is clear evidence to suggest that, prior to 1971, the freedom to hire and fire was interpreted by some employers with less than reasonable regard for either the fairness or humanity of their decisions. In one sense, therefore, the 1971 Act introduced some degree of balance in such instances. In many organisations, its effect was little more than to endorse statutorily arrangements already in existence.

An examination of cases heard by tribunals in recent years demonstrates that some employers, despite legislation, still adopt a cavalier attitude in their relationships with employees. It is important to emphasise, however, that the law in no way precludes such behaviour. Rather it offers some degree of compensation for employees concerned. In no sense is an employer deprived of his essential freedom to dismiss.

One of the specific objectives of the Employment Act 1980 was claimed to be the 'restoration of balance' between employers and employees. Among its provisions were a number dealing with unfair dismissal. The principal effect of these was to alter dramatically the onus of proof. Instead of the employer having to show that his action was fair, it is now for the tribunal to consider the matter 'in accordance with equity and the substantial merits of the case'. What the practical consequences of this will be, has still to be seen. However, even before the new provisions, an increase in the qualifying period for protection had resulted in a decrease in tribunal cases of between 23 and 25 per cent. Of cases heard, in only 28 per cent were employees successful. Statistically the scales appear, therefore, to be far from weighted in favour of employees.

Recommended reading

ACAS, *Code of Practice No. 1: Disciplinary practice and procedures for employment*, HMSO, 1977.

IPM, *Disciplinary Procedures and Practice—Information Report 28*, IPM, 1979.

Selwyn, N. M., *Law of Employment*, Butterworths, 1980 or later edition.

Slade, E. A., *Tolley's Employment Handbook*, 2nd ed., Tolley Publishing Co. Ltd, 1979 with 1980 supplement (or later edition).

Pratt K. J. and Bennett S. G., *Elements of Personnel Management*, Gee & Co. Ltd, 1979 (Chap. 24).

15 Redundancy

Introduction

Redundancy is a topic which has dominated the employment scene in recent years. It must be remembered, however, that it is not simply an invention of the late 1970s and early 1980s but it is an inevitable problem in any free-market economy. To some degree the probability and consequences of its incidence may be reduced by skilful manpower planning. However, recent experience has shown clearly how even the best prepared and most resilient of organisations may be confronted by the need for reductions of its workforce.

Questions asked by examiners appear to focus on two aspects of the subject – the legislative provisions and the practical managerial considerations when planning and implementing redundancies. At first sight these appear very different: in fact they overlap to a considerable degree. Statute now establishes very firm guidelines regarding the handling of such situations and it is on this basis that any adequate answer is likely to be founded.

Statutory provisions relating to redundancy are found for the first time in the Redundancy Payments Act 1965 (RPA). Before this no right to compensation existed except in cases where a breach of contract of employment could be demonstrated: the RPA introduced more general rights to compensation – these are discussed below. Guidance on redundancy policies and procedures was provided by the 1972 Code of Industrial Practice, the provisions of which were largely formalised by their integration in the Employment Protection Act 1975 and subsequently in the Employment Protection (Consolidation) Act 1978. Under the 1978 Act an employee is redundant if he is dismissed due to:

1 his employer ceasing or preparing to cease to carry on the business for the purposes of which the employee was employed; or
2 his employer ceasing or proposing to cease to carry on that business in the place where the employee was employed; or
3 the requirements of that business for employees to carry out work of a particular kind, or for them to carry out that work in the place where they are so employed, have ceased or diminished or are expected to cease or diminish.

Sample examination question

What major legal and managerial considerations must be taken into account when the need arises to make redundant 10% of a factory

workforce, either by a scheme of early retirement or by laying off
most recent recruits?   (*ACA*)

Key points

1 Legal considerations will include the provisions of the Redundancy
  Payments Act 1965 and the Employment Protection Act 1975, the
  former now largely encompassed in the Employment Protection
  (Consolidation) Act 1978.

2 A summary of the provisions of such statutes with particular attention to: rights to compensation, notification of redundancies, consultation with independent trade unions, time off to look for work,
  offers of alternative employment.

3 The risk of unfair dismissal claims due to non-adherance to agreed
  procedures or discriminatory behaviour.

4 An analysis of the two proposed schemes for the selection of redundant staff: early retirement or period of service.

5 Non-statutory responsibilities: assistance to employees in finding
  alternative employment.

6 Possible alternatives to redundancy, eg short-time working, lay-offs
  etc.

7 The possibility of industrial action.

Suggested answer

Legal provisions relating to a redundancy proposal such as that outlined in the
question are to be found in the Redundancy Payments Act 1965 and the
Employment Protection Act 1975. The former now falls largely under the
general umbrella of the Employment Protection (Consolidation) Act 1978.
While not strictly law, the Code of Industrial Relations Practice 1972 also
recommends policies and procedures to be adopted in such circumstances.

With the exception of certain specific groups, eg those under 18, or past the
statutory retirement age, all redundant employees with at least 104 weeks'
service with their current employer are entitled to redundancy pay. Such pay is
determined by length of service and age at redundancy.

In each case compensation is limited to the last 20 years of service and a
national weekly wage determined from time to time by the Secretary of State for
Employment. A portion of such statutory compensation may be recovered by
the employer from a government redundancy fund (currently 41%); however,
no recovery may be made either in respect of ex-gratia payments or payments in
excess of the statutory figure – any such additional costs must be borne by the
employer.

Where more than 10 employees are to be made redundant, the employer is required to give advance notice to the Department of Employment in accordance with a timetable laid down by the Secretary of State. Currently this requires that if 10 or more are to be made redundant during a period of 30 days, at least 60 days' notice must be given. If more than 100 are to be made redundant over a period of 90 days, the requisite period of notice is also 90 days. Failure to give proper notice may result in loss of rebate or a fine.

Where an independent trade union is recognised in respect of the workers or group of workers concerned, then the employer is also required to consult with that trade union. Where more than 10 employees are affected, consultation must similarly commence in accordance with the timetable outlined above. This rule applies whether or not the employees concerned are union members. Failure to consult may result in a tribunal making a protective award of up to 90 days' pay to appropriate employees, whether still employed or not. Exceptionally, an employer may escape this provision where he is able to demonstrate that it was not practicable for him to comply fully with statutory requirements. As a basis for consultation, information must be made available regarding:

1 The reasons for the proposed redundancies;
2 The number and descriptions of employees affected;
3 The total number of such employees at the location in question;
4 The proposed method for selecting redundant employees;
5 The proposed method and timing for implementing the redundancies.

Subsequent to such consultation, it will be necessary to arrange for the announcement of individual redundancies and the interview of the staff concerned. While the latter step is not always included, it is infinitely better than a bald written statement. An appeals procedure is commonly provided for; often to a joint management-union committee. Detailed provisions relating to holiday entitlement, periods of notice, fringe benefits etc will also need to be formulated.

An employee who has been given notice of redundancy and has two years' service is entitled to reasonable time off with pay to find other work or training. If refused, he may apply to an industrial tribunal for redress. Alternatively, it may be that an employer is able to offer suitable employment elsewhere within the organisation. Under such circumstances, the employee is not entitled to compensation; instead his old and new jobs are treated as an unbroken period of service. Such alternative work must be appropriate bearing in mind the employee's previous post and if necessary this may be determined by reference to an industrial tribunal. In any case, both parties are entitled to a minimum of four weeks' trial period, during which time either may terminate the new contract, the employee then normally being considered redundant as if the new job had never existed. Entitlement to compensation may, however, be lost where an employee unreasonably terminates his new contract.

In the question, two alternative means of selecting staff for redundancy are listed. Whichever is adopted it is important that it be clearly communicated to those concerned and strictly adhered to by management. Whereas redundancy is normally considered a fair basis for dismissal, an unfair dismissal claim may arise in instances where either there is evidence of selection on a discriminatory basis or where an agreed procedure for the selection of redundant staff is not implemented. Each of the means of selection has its own benefits and problems.

So far as laying-off the most recent recruits is concerned (often called 'LIFO' – 'last in, first out'), the method has to recommend it the probability of minimum cost and maximum trade union support. On the other hand, it may well result in the organisation losing younger, more vigorous workers and indeed, takes no account of individual skill, efficiency or potential. Early retirement, while often resulting in the loss to the organisation of highly skilled and experienced staff, may very well be welcomed by those eligible for it, thus minimising problems of adverse employee reaction. Its acceptability, however, is inevitably dictated by the generosity of the terms under which it is offered and its short-term cost is thus almost certain to be considerable.

In addition to its statutory duties, it is often argued that management has further social and moral responsibilities to those about to be made redundant. Clearly of paramount value will be attempts to assist staff in finding new work. This may involve liaison with the appropriate government departments or, as some employers have done, involve setting-up job-hunting teams to chase vacancies with other organisations. Staff will also often require counselling regarding the financial and personal consequences of redundancy as well as how best to prepare themselves for finding new employment.

Although from the question it appears that the redundancies are inevitable, it is both socially and organisationally desirable that management should continue to seek alternative courses of action. These might include the elimination of overtime, short-time working, lay-offs, producing for stock etc. At a time when an organisation is patently facing serious difficulties, some might think it illogical that the workforce would further endanger their jobs through industrial action. Illogical or not, it is apparent that such action is a typical response to the announcement of redundancies. While in no way guaranteeing co-operation, management's apparent willingness to consult fully and to consider alternative courses of action may at least minimise the likelihood of such behaviour.

Further examination questions

1 Due to the present economic situation, it is likely that a number of administrative staff in your organisation will be declared redundant in the next few months.

   Draw up details of a policy to be followed of the most equitable method of dealing with this redundancy situation.   (*ICSA*)

2 Computerisation and the ever-increasing number of mergers has brought the very real threat of redundancies much nearer. Outline what you consider are the essential features of any redundancy agreement.   (*CBSI*)

3 Indicate the practical problems which a personnel manager might have to overcome in dealing with a major collective (ie not purely individual) redundancy.   (*ICSA*)

4 In what ways may an organisation plan to avoid unnecessary redundancies, and ease those which are inevitable?   (*IAM*)

5 Under what circumstances does the law require an employer to consult with Trade Unions? (*IPM*)

General comments on questions

Question 1, like most of the further sample questions, requires an essentially practical approach. Nevertheless, in dealing with it, you must be aware of the statutory requirements and procedures prescribed by statute and outlined above. The question refers to a 'policy' to be followed. In our opinion, what the examiner requires is a more specific identification of the matters which will need consideration. The question indicates that the redundancies are still only a possibility. In this instance, it is therefore probably appropriate at least to mention those measures which may be considered as means of avoiding or minimising actual redundancies. Specific mention should be made of the advantages to be derived from finding alternative employment opportunities elsewhere within the organisation. A programme should be formulated for both consultation with staff representatives and the announcement of general and detailed arrangements. The statutory timetable for this is dealt with in the suggested answer above. Determination of a basis for the selection of redundant staff will be a prime consideration, and the examiner when referring to an 'equitable method' probably expects some demonstration of the advantages and problems associated with the alternative selection criteria. Arrangements for the communication of redundancy to individual employees, appeals procedures and efforts to assist staff in finding new work will also require discussion. An answer developed along basically similar lines would also be appropriate for **Questions 2 and 3**; though in **Question 3**, it is probable that the examiner has in mind the likelihood of industrial action and the ways in which it may best be avoided. As in so many cases, no guaranteed recipe for success is preferred, but essential elements, as mentioned above, would appear to be maximum possible period of notice, early and full consultation, the willingness to seek and consider alternatives, a clear and practical demonstration of concern for the future of the employees concerned and, wherever possible, compensation in excess of that demanded by statute.

Question 4, although requiring some re-statement of the above, is very different in emphasis. In dealing with the first part of the question it is necessary to discuss the way in which effective manpower planning and a constant review of manpower requirements may aid an organisation in avoiding unnecessary redundancies. A discussion of further preventitive measures, eg 'freezing' recruitment, short-time working, reduction of overtime etc, is also required. In dealing with the latter half of the question, the emphasis is again on the practical assistance which may be given to redundant employees in finding new employment and adjusting to their changed social and financial circumstances. This is yet another occasion where practical examples from your own experience or reading will add significant weight to your answer.

Question 5 is very different from the others and at first sight is not obviously about redundancy at all. Nevertheless, if we are to interpret the question strictly, it would appear that the only instance in which an employer is legally required to consult with a trade union is in relation to the proposed redundancy of an employee or employees of a class in respect of which an independent trade union is recognised. The areas for consultation are indicated in the suggested answer. It must be noted that where a trade union representation is rejected, the reasons for its rejection must be given. It is worthwhile reiterating, however, that the employer's duty is to *consult*. While failure to consult may render the employer liable to a claim for compensation, so too may the incautious adoption of union proposals regarding selection procedures. In each case management must ensure that whatever arrangements are determined, they must be free from discrimination and in line with any previously agreed procedure or customary arrangement.

Recommended reading

Selwyn, N. M., *Law of Employment*, Butterworths, 1980 (Chap. 10).

Roberts, D., 'Before and After Redundancy: Company Policy and Reality', *Personnel Management*, July 1977.

IPM, *Executive Redundancy – Information Report 30*, IPM, 1979.

Daniel, W. W., *Whatever Happened to the Workers in Woolwich? A Survey of Redundancy in SE London*, PEP, 1972.

Pratt, K. J. and Bennett, S. G., *Elements of Personnel Management*, Gee & Company Ltd, 1979. (Chap. 25).

16   Legal aspects of employment

Introduction

If one examines the development of personnel management, a salient feature is the plethora of government regulation and codification of the employer/employee relationship introduced during the past twenty years. Indeed, there are now few aspects of that relationship which are not, in one way or another, subject to the law, associated regulations or codes of practice. In this age of consumerism and rapid mass communication systems, employees and their representatives are increasingly well informed about their substantial statutory employment rights and their employers' obligations. Thus no manager, but in particular no personnel manager, can hope to fulfil his responsibilities effectively without a good knowledge of the subject. This importance is reflected in the frequency with which questions requiring answers with a legal basis appear not only in specifically personnel management papers, but also in the more general management papers set by many professional bodies.

As indicated above, there are now few aspects of the employer/employee relationship and thus the personnel management functions which are not in some way affected by statutory provisions; indeed in some instances, eg dismissal procedures, personnel practice and the relevant legal provisions have effectively fused with each other. Inevitably therefore there is some overlap of material dealt with in this section with that discussed elsewhere.

As in other examinations which you may have sat which required legal or quasi-legal answers, two particular points of examination technique are worthy of note. Examiners will appreciate answers in which some attempt is made to use 'real life' illustrations to demonstrate the operation, efficiency or inadequacy of legal provisions. Secondly, when quoting a statute it is customary, at least on the first occasion, to quote the full title and date: when revising, ensure that you have accurately committed these to memory.

Sample examination question

In what major ways has British legislation attempted to pursue social fairness in employment over the past twelve years?   (*ACA*)

Key points

NB: The question refers to the 'past twelve years'. Marks will not be gained for answers based on earlier statutes.

1 A brief definition of what is understood by 'social fairness in employment' – essentially the law attempts to protect groups otherwise liable to discrimination or disadvantage.

2 Most recent employment law in one way or another contributes to this objective. However, specific contributions are made by the Sex Discrimination Act 1975, the Race Relations Act 1976, the Equal Pay Act 1970, the Employment Protection Act 1975, the Employment Protection (Consolidation) Act 1978.

3 A summary of the provisions of the Sex Discrimination, Race Relations and Equal Pay Acts.

4 The Employment Protection (Consolidation) Act brings together a range of protective statute and establishes various employee rights, eg guarantee payments, suspension on medical grounds, insolvency of an employer. Salient provisions have to do with trade union membership, pregnancy, dismissal, redundancy.

5 A *brief summary* of the law relating to the employee protection aspects of the trade union membership, pregnancy, dismissal and redundancy provisions.

6 In all the above instances rights may be enforced by application to an industrial tribunal and thereafter by appeal to the Employment Appeal Tribunal. As a long-term means of establishing fairness such externally policed arrangements may, however, be of limited value.

Suggested answer

In order to answer this question it is first of all necessary to clarify the meaning of 'social fairness in employment', since it is an expression capable of multifarious interpretation. An examination of employment legislation during the past twelve years reveals a recurring theme: the protection of workers individually or in groups who might otherwise be discriminated against or placed at a disadvantage by others, and in particular by employers. It is presumably in this sense that the expression is used.

Employment statute now extends to virtually all aspects of the employer/employee relationship, and inherent in most is at least some element which might be interpreted as contributing to 'social fairness'. Thus for example, the Employment and Training Act 1973, by establishing a more orderly national training structure and by encouraging industrial training, might be viewed in this way. Other statutes are more clearly orientated towards this objective: in particular the Sex Discrimination Act 1975, the Race Relations Act 1976, the Equal Pay Act 1970, the Employment Protection Act 1975 and the Employment Protection (Consolidation) Act 1978.

So far as the Sex Discrimination and Race Relations Acts are concerned, each sets out to achieve a similar objective and logically each follows a similar pattern. Discrimination, with certain exceptions, is outlawed on sex or marital grounds under the former, and on racial, colour, nationality, ethnic or national origin grounds under the latter. Both direct and indirect discrimination are covered by each. Direct discrimination arises where a person treats another less favourably on sex or race grounds, whereas indirect consists of treatment which may be described as equal in a formal sense, but is discriminatory in its effect on one particular sex, marital or racial group. Thus it would normally be unlawful to discriminate in the arrangements made for determining who shall be offered a job, in the terms on which employment is offered, or by refusing or deliberately omitting to offer a person employment. Once an employee is appointed it is similarly unlawful to discriminate in relation to transfer, training, promotion or to any other benefits, facilities or services. As indicated above, certain exceptions apply; principally those dealing with 'genuine occupational qualifications' and employment in private households. Other specific exceptions apply under each of the Acts.

Introduced in 1970, but coming into force in 1975, the Equal Pay Act complements the Sex Discrimination Act. The 1970 Act provides that, where a woman is employed on work of a similar nature to that of a man, or in a job which has been given an equal value to a man's job under job evaluation, then that woman is entitled to the same rate of pay and other terms of employment as the man.

In 1978, the Employment Protection (Consolidation) Act (EPCA) was introduced. As its title suggests, the Act brought together a whole range of statutes intended to protect employees, eg sections of the Employment Protection Act, the Contracts of Employment Act and the Redundancy Payments Acts. *Inter alia*, the Act provides for guarantee payments where employees are not provided with work; payment for up to 26 weeks where an employee is suspended from work on medical grounds, and some degree of financial protection where an employer becomes insolvent. Additionally four major areas of provision are contained – those dealing with trade union membership, pregnancy, dismissal and redundancy.

In relation to trade union membership, an employee has the right not to have action taken against him by his employer which would prevent or deter him from becoming a member of an independent trade union or from taking part in its activities. Additionally, an employer may not compel an employee to become a member of a non-independent trade union.

Provided she has the appropriate period of service, the Act provides that an employee who is dismissed because she is pregnant, will normally be treated as unfairly dismissed unless she is incapable of doing her job or for her to continue in the job would involve breaking the law. In both instances dismissal will still be unfair where the employee in question was not offered a suitable available vacant post. In addition to the right not to be dismissed, pregnant employees also become eligible for maternity pay payable by the employer, and have the right to return to work within 29 weeks of the date of confinement. Although the Employment Act 1980 has provided some margin of employer discretion so far as the precise job is concerned to which the employee returns, nevertheless an employee is entitled to return to work on terms and conditions no less favourable than would have applied had she not been absent. In order to qualify for such rights, an employee must safisfy certain period of service requirements and give notice of her intention to return in accordance with a timetable laid down by the Employment Act 1980.

So far as 'fairness' is concerned, the aspect which appears likely to be of principal concern to most employees is that their employer should not on the basis of whim, fancy or some other equally invalid motive be able to terminate their employment. Summarised very briefly, the 1978 Act brings together provisions originally found in the Industrial Relations Act 1971, the Trade Union and Labour Relations Act 1974 and the Employment Protection Act 1975 to create a situation where, if an employee, with at least 52 weeks of service, feels that he has been unfairly dismissed, then he has right of application to an industrial tribunal which may either require his re-instatement, re-engagement or award compensation consisting of a basic award and, in addition, a compensatory award based on the employee's loss arising out of the dismissal. Where an employer fails to comply with an order for reinstatement or re-engagement or where it is shown that the reason for the unfair dismissal had to do with union membership, race or sex discrimination, then a further additional award may be made. Indeed, where the reason for dismissal has to do with trade union membership, the employee concerned may apply to a tribunal for interim relief pending the outcome of the case. The Act further provides that all employees who have completed 26 weeks' employment have the right to receive from their employer a written statement of the reasons for their dismissal, such a statement to be supplied within 14 days.

Finally, as indicated above, the 1978 Act encompasses most of the provisions of the Redundancy Payments Act 1965. Again, summarised very briefly, the Act provides that employees with at least two years' service, and whom it is intended to make redundant, shall be entitled to compensation. Such compensation is to be calculated in relation to employees' age and period of service. Similarly an employee who has been laid off or kept on short time for several weeks may be entitled to a redundancy payment. Statutory periods of notice of redundancy must be given, consultation with independent trade unions must normally take place where they exist, and employees entitled to compensation are also entitled to reasonable time off with pay to seek new work.

It is through such employee rights as those outlined above that various governments have sought to achieve the fairness in employment mentioned in the question. Such rights are all very well, but are pointless unless capable of enforcement. In respect of all the above, as in the case of unfair dismissal, an employee who feels that he is unfairly treated normally has the right to apply to an industrial tribunal and if necessary thereafter to the Employment Appeal Tribunal.

Clearly such measures as those outlined above have done much to establish a balance in the employers/employee relationship. However, whether or not such a relationship can, in the long term, rely on externally policed rules and regulations must be a matter for speculation.

Further examination questions

1 List, with brief explanations, the items which must according to current legislation be included in a standard letter of appointment and contract of employment.   (*CBSI*)

2 What rights do trade union representatives have, under current legislation, to information from the employer? *(IPM)*

3 The Employment Protection Act 1975 introduced the concept of 'constructive dismissal'. Explain precisely what is meant by this term. As Personnel Manager, what procedures would you recommend to your society to ensure that constructive unfair dismissals do not take place? *(CBSI)*

4 In relation to 'picketing', what does the law say is permissible conduct, and what areas of difficulty are highlighted by picketing activities of the past decade? *(IPM)*

5 How is the 1975 Sex Discrimination Act likely to affect personnel policies and procedures of companies and other organisations in the coming years? *(ICSA)*

6 What new rights have been established by the Employment Protection Act 1975 for female employees who become pregnant? What particular problems do these rights cause for the employer? *(CBSI)*

7 In the last ten years a considerable amount of legislation affecting the employment of staff has been passed by Parliament. How would you, as a newly appointed Personnel Officer in a Society of £100 million assets and 25 branches, define for your senior management colleagues the personnel policies which you feel are necessary to cope with this law?

Answers should be in note form and must refer to the basic requirements of current legislation. *(CBSI)*

8 Discuss with appropriate examples the changing impact of the law on the personnel function. *(ICSA)*

General comments on questions

Question 1 requires a straightforward answer to a straightforward question – what are the items that must be included in a letter of appointment or contract of employment? Originally prescribed by the Contracts of Employment Act 1963, such items are now listed in the Employment Protection (Consolidation) Act 1978. Whatever the form of statement adopted, ie letter, formal contract, or statement in lieu of contract, the following information must be given:
1 Identification of the parties to the contract.
2 The date when the employment began; and whether or not any employment with a previous employer counts as part of the employee's continuous employment.
3 The scale, rate or method of calculating remuneration and the intervals at which remuneration is to be paid.
4 Terms and conditions relating to hours of work, holidays and holiday pay, sick pay and pension rights.
5 Periods of notice which the employee must give or be given.

6 The title of the job which the employee is employed to do.
7 Whether a contracting-out certificate in respect of the State Pension Scheme is in force in respect of the employment concerned.
8 Details of any disciplinary rules applicable to the employee.
9 Details of persons to whom the employee may apply if he is dissatisfied with any disciplinary decision relating to him or wishes to seek redress of a grievance relating to his employment. The steps to be taken in such cases must also be explained.

It should be noted that the Act excludes certain groups of employees from the above provisions, eg Crown employees, part-time staff working less than 16 hours per week, the spouse of the employer. The required information, in whatever form, must be given not later than the end of the thirteenth week of employment and any subsequent changes notified within one month.

In connection with this question it must be noted that although the examiner refers to a 'letter of appointment and contract of employment', the two are not the same nor necessarily contained in the same document. A contract of employment may or may not be committed to paper; a letter of appointment may or may not be issued; neither is required by law. What is required is that, whatever the means of forming the contract of employment, within the first 13 weeks a written statement in some form containing the information outlined above must be issued to an employee.

The provision of information is also the subject of **Question 2**. Under current law there are three main areas where trade union representatives are entitled to receive information from employers. These are in relation to redundancy, health and safety and collective bargaining. Information requirements regarding proposed redundancies are to be found in the suggested answer to the sample examination question in the section of this book dealing with redundancy, but briefly these have to do with the reasons for the redundancies, the number of staff affected and management's proposed plan of action. Such rights are provided by the Employment Protection Act 1975. So far as health and safety are concerned, the Safety Representatives and Safety Committees Regulations 1977 entitle safety representatives appointed by recognised trade unions to receive information including:

1 Details of plans and performance of the organisation in so far as they relate to health and safety at work.
2 Technical data about hazards to health and safety and precautions necessary to eliminate or reduce them.
3 Records and statistics of accidents, dangerous recurrences or notifiable diseases.
4 Any other relevant matter, including the results of any measurements taken in the course of checking the effectiveness of health and safety arrangements.

In connection with such information it should be noted that certain exceptions exist for confidential items and security.

Undoubtedly the most contentious aspect of disclosure of information is that provided for under the Employment Protection Act 1975. This imposes a duty on employers to disclose to representatives of independent trade unions information for the purpose of collective bargaining. Such information must be normally in the employer's possession, relate to the employing organisation and be such that without it a trade union representative would be impeded to a material extent in bargaining. Where a trade union considers that an employer has failed to disclose appropriate information, it may make a complaint to the Central Arbitration Committee (CAC), which, if the matter cannot be settled by conciliation, may require disclosure. Where an employer continues to fail to release information, the CAC may make an award relating to terms and conditions of employment against the employer.

While no duty is imposed to disclose specific information, it is apparent from ACAS Code of Practice 2, that very little information relating to corporate policy or performance is considered inappropriate for disclosure. Nevertheless certain examples are identified where the possibility of substantial organisational injury might result from publication.

Question 3 begins by inviting you to define the term 'constructive dismissal'. As indicated in the question, the concept was established by the Employment Protection Act 1975 (EPA). Initially it was interpreted as meaning any situation in which an employee was not dismissed, but felt bound to resign because of the unreasonable behaviour of his employer. Such an interpretation led to a whole series of sometimes extraordinary tribunal decisions. The situation was eventually clarified in *Western Excavating Ltd v. Sharp* (1978). Here it was held that it was not enough to demonstrate that an employer had behaved unreasonably; rather, that the employer's conduct amounted to a breach of contract of employment.

In avoiding such a situation, techniques and procedures discussed elsewhere in this book will clearly be of value. Well established and communicated disciplinary and grievance procedures will ensure both that mischevious claims may be disproved and that cases of victimisation may be identified at an early stage. Effective staff appraisal schemes will similarly aid an upward flow of information, often revealing problems at a stage in their development where a solution may be more readily discovered. For a discussion of the characteristics of such procedures you are referred to the sections on staff appraisal (7), dismissal (14) and redundancy (15).

Question 4 similarly seeks an answer which combines legal knowledge with an appreication of its practical application: some might say in this instance, its impractical application! Picketing, not surprisingly perhaps, is an aspect of industrial relations which, like the 'closed shop', is regularly and variously reviewed by politicians. The most recent of such reviews is contained in the Employment Act 1980. This states that it is lawful for a person in contemplation or furtherance of a trade dispute to attend:

a at or near his own place of work; or

b if he is an official of a trade union, at or near the place of work of a member of that union whom he is accompanying and whom he represents;

for the purpose only of peacefully obtaining or communicating information or peacefully persuading any person to work or to abstain from working. So long as this provision is strictly complied with, any person taking such action enjoys statutory immunity from civil legal proceedings.

Three points should be noted in particular:

a No immunity is granted against criminal proceedings.

b The Act refers to picketing 'at or near' the employee's 'own place of work'.

c The law permits only *peaceful* picketing.

In the second part of the question, the examiner asks that you discuss areas of difficulty highlighted by picketing activity during the past decade. Clearly what he is inviting you to do is to contrast the legal rules with what may be observed to happen in practice. In connection with this, let us again emphasise two important points. The examiner will be impressed by students who are able to illustrate their answers with examples drawn from recent events; it is important therefore that you keep up to date by reading newspapers and the appropriate journals. The examiner will not be impressed, however, by students who take the opportunity in this sort of question to launch into dogmatic political arguments, of whatever complexion.

What areas will the examiner expect you to discuss? Despite the existence of a relatively clear legal framework, recent picketing practice has raised a number of questions about the adequacy of such provisions. It is clear that much unlawful 'secondary' picketing as defined in the Employment Act 1980 and the use of mobile squads of 'flying pickets' continues. Equally a continuing number of picketing incidents are characterised by intimidation by large numbers of pickets, sometimes escalating into overtly violent behaviour, the forced halting of vehicles, clashes with the police, etc. Instances such as the 'Shrewsbury Two' following the introduction of the Industrial Relations Act 1971 have revealed how, when attempts have been made to implement the law, the result has often been the precipitation of even greater difficulty than that which previously existed. In a broader context it is probably worthwhile to consider to what extent greater reliance ought to be placed in this and other instances on voluntary codes of practice, etc.

Reference has already been made in the suggested answer to the provisions of the Sex Discrimination Act 1975. **Question 5** asks in what ways the provisions of the Act are likely to affect personnel policies and procedures. In addition to the areas already dealt with above, it is probably appropriate to attempt a brief evaluation of the Act's effects to date, together with those of its associated act, the Equal Pay Act 1970. This reveals a somewhat chequered picture. It is apparent that both Acts have succeeded in narrowing the gap so far as differences in employment practice based purely on sex or marital status are concerned. On the other hand a significant margin still exists between average male and female earnings, tribunal hearings suggest that at least a proportion of employers continue to seek ways around the law, and women achieving managerial status are considered newsworthy. So far as the unions are concerned, the story is not very different: strikes have been called because of management proposals to equalise male and female terms and conditions, unions have, with notable exceptions, been unusually reserved in pursuing statutory rights and, despite a growing female membership, the number of female union officials is still disproportionately low.

Question 6 deals with statutory rights attaching to female employees who become pregnant. Although the question refers to the Employment Protection Act 1975, now contained in the Employment Protection Consolidation Act 1978 (EPCA), which originally established such rights, the Employment Act 1980 has significantly amended the earlier provisions. Under the EPCA a woman who, eleven weeks before her anticipated confinement has been employed by her employer for at least two years and has continued in her employment up to that date, is entitled:

a to retain her job, pregnancy itself not being a valid reason for dismissal;
b to return to her job up to 29 weeks after her baby is born;

c to receive maternity pay covering the first six weeks of her absence due to the birth or anticipated birth of her baby.

Where a woman is dismissed for reasons of pregnancy or her employer refuses to allow her return, and she is qualified to do so, then she has a right of application to an industrial tribunal which may require her reinstatement or make a cash award.

The Employment Act 1980 amends such rights both procedurally and substantively. A major modification is that where an employer employs five or fewer employees and it is not reasonably practicable either to allow an employee to return or to offer suitable alternative work, then he is not obliged to take her back and she will have no claim. Similarly, any employer who cannot practicably permit an employee to return to her old job may offer suitable alternative employment. Where this is accepted or unreasonably refused by the employee, she again loses her rights.

Procedurally the 1980 Act is very much more onerous than earlier provisions. Three weeks before her absence begins an employee must inform her employer in writing:

a that she will be absent because of her pregnancy or confinement;
b that she intends to return to work; and
c of the anticipated or actual date of her confinement.

Seven weeks after the notified date of confinement, an employer may ask an employee to confirm her intention to return. A failure to reply to the employer's request leads to the loss of the right to return. In his request for confirmation the employer must explain such consequences. When the employee eventually wishes to return, she must give written notice of that fact. Either employer or employee may, under certain circumstances, delay her return up to a further maximum of four weeks. In addition to such rights, it should be noted that the Employment Protection (Consolidation) Act 1978 provides for pregnant employees, on the advice of doctor, midwife or health visitor, to have time off with pay for ante-natal care.

So far as problems caused for the employer are concerned, the most important is undoubtedly how to arrange for the completion of the absent employee's work. While provision exists for the appointment of a temporary replacement, this will involve the organisation in additional recruitment and training costs and the negotiation of temporary contracts of employment. In instances where some skill attaches to the job concerned, such temporary arrangements may prove wholly impracticable or uneconomic. Some alternative means may thus have to be found, perhaps involving temporary additional payments to other staff. Additionally administrative procedures will have to be established both to pay maternity benefits and to correspond with absent employees regarding their planned return. While such problems may prove relatively minor in the majority of cases, the problems are clearly very much more involved where a key member of staff or management is concerned.

In answering questions such as **Question 7**, it is important that you observe very carefully any 'cut-off' date indicated by the examiner. In this instance he is interested in legislation introduced over the past ten years. At the time of writing (1982), this would therefore include such statutes as the Contracts of Employment Act 1972, the Employment and Training Act 1973, the Trade Union and Labour Relations Act 1974, the Health and Safety at Work, etc Act 1974, the Employment Protection Act 1975, the Race Relations

Act 1976, the Equal Pay Act 1970, the Sex Discrimination Act 1975, the Employment Protection (Consolidation) Act 1978, the Employment Act 1980. So far as areas of policy are concerned, a variety of categories are possible; for example: manpower planning and control (including recruitment, selection, dismissal, redundancy), education and training, working conditions, industrial relations. Whatever the categories decided upon, it is essential that you strike a balance between revealing your knowledge of the law on the one hand, while on the other demonstrating its practical consequence so far as the need for policy formulation is concerned. You should note in particular that the examiner requires the answer to be in note form.

Question 8 requires a very different sort of answer. Although the question asks for examples of the way in which the law affects the personnel function, what the examiner does *not* want is an illustrated list of statutes of the kind that constitutes a sound basis for an answer to the sample examination question or Question 7 above. Rather he requires a discussion of the way in which such statutes have modified the nature of the personnel function's environment and tasks. This has already been considered elsewhere (see Section 2 on the Personnel Function and the Role of the Personnel Manager) and so it is not intended to go into detail here. Nevertheless your answer should consider *inter alia* the way in which statute has translated individual worker privileges and employer initiatives into universal rights with a consequent redistribution of aspects of management's traditional authority into the hands of workers, their representatives and assorted government agencies and tribunals. In consequence the role of the personnel function increasingly has to do with the implementation and interpretation of externally prescribed policies. While not yet legally enforceable, various statutes have combined to enhance both the status of collective agreements and that of those who negotiate them (see Question 2 above). Such a change has similar consequences for the personnel role, as well as demanding improved communications systems – another area of personnel expertise. Thomason suggests that the combination of such factors will require executive action from a previously advisory function in three ways:

a as a repository of knowledge as to the rules which apply;
b as an adviser or trainer of line management in the application of these rules;
c as a monitor of the actual application of the rules.
(Thomason, G., *A Textbook of Personnel Management*, IPM, 2nd ed., 1981)

Recommended reading

This is an area where it is notoriously difficult to recommend reading to students, since textbooks date so rapidly as new legislation is introduced. On a more positive note, however, the introduction of new employment statutes is generally followed both by a stream of analytical articles in professional journals and by the publication of (usually free) guides to the new law published by the Department of Employment, ACAS etc. These are normally available on demand from either the local or head office of the agency concerned. The following more traditional texts are, however, recommended:

Selwyn, N. M., *Law of Employment*, Butterworths, 1980, or a later edition.
Slade, E. A., *Tolley's Employment Handbook*, 2nd ed., Tolley Publishing Co. Ltd, 1979 with 1980 supplement, or a later edition.

17 Change and organisation development

Introduction

Although the title of this section may appear somewhat abstract and little to do with the recognised functions of personnel management, we make no apology for its inclusion. The number of examination questions in this area reflects the importance which many managers and organisations attach to the challenge of change and the problems which accompany it.

Change can, of course, take many forms and may arise from inside or outside of an organisation. There are times when management must adapt to change and those when the initiative should be theirs. Virtually all changes to an organisation will have some effect upon the workforce. It could be said, therefore, that the personnel manager should be a major influence upon the management of change. This certainly appears to be the view of some commentators. Charles Margerison states: 'The personnel and training specialist spent most of this time in selection interviews, administration, liaising with training boards and occasionally, instructing. Now this role is being extended. Personnel and training specialists are becoming more involved with the management and organisation aspects of the business. The job is in a state of rapid evolution. . . .'

Similarly, Bristow, Carby and Thakur contend that: 'While many of the policy decisions on major issues such as pay, productivity and participation may be made elsewhere, it will usually be the personnel department which will be primarily involved in helping the organisation cope with changes in these and similar areas.'

The above views may or may not be shared by examiners, but the ability to put forward the arguments in an informed and authoritative manner is crucial to success in this area. Apart from a knowledge of the skills and techniques available to a personnel manager, you will require a grounding of the principles of organisation development (OD). Literature on this subject is now widely available from both American and British authors. You will also need to draw upon your knowledge of current affairs and contemporary developments in order to provide appropriate background material.

Sample examination question

Resistance to change is common, both at an organisational and individual level. Comment on the reasons for this and suggest policies which might minimise non-productive resistance.   (*IAM*)

Key points

 1 Outline pressures upon management to introduce change and give
   examples.

 2 Main reasons for resistance – irrational and rational reactions –
   individual and group anxieties.

 3 Methods of managing change. Research findings and organisation
   development (OD) techniques.

Suggested answer

It is the job of management to design a structure and system of operations
which will produce goods and/or services as efficiently as possible. In order for
the organisation to be successful in terms of productivity and profit management, it must be able to harness the skills and knowledge of the workforce to an
optimum level. The continuing success of the organisation will, however, be
dependent upon its ability to predict events in the external environment and
influence the organisation's response to these. As a result of economic, technical
or political pressures, it may be necessary to make changes ranging from a major
reorganisation to minor modifications affecting only a few staff.

Probably the most significant and continuous pressure upon the management of a commercial organisation is that of the market place. As a result of
changing demands and competition it will be necessary to modify or replace
products or to find ways of producing them more cheaply than competitors can.
This will inevitably result in changed work methods and variations in the relationships between different groups and individuals.

Resistance to the introduction of change may arise for a whole variety of
reasons but it can often be attributed to management failing to understand and
allow for the anxieties and uncertainties which change may arouse. These may
be emotional (due to unfounded fears about redundancy, loss of status, etc) or
rational (concerned with matters of incentive, reward or training facilities). The
resultant resistance may involve individuals, small groups or whole workforces.

Ever since Hawthorne, the enormous amount of research into work groups
has shown time and again that they develop certain behavioural norms and attitudes. Any change which threatens the group or attempts to alter its custom and
practice may well meet strong resistance. Individuals will develop firm ideas of
their role and status within an organisation and may resent attempts to vary the
amount of control which they have over the work situation. At a wider level the
resistance may become institutionalised through the action of trade unions or
staff associations. They will have clear ideas about the 'rights' of their membership and will refuse to see these altered without a suitable *quid pro quo*.

If resistance to change is to be minimised in order to avoid major loss of production or efficiency, management would do well to recognise the social and
psychological factors referred to above. Having recognised them, what policies
would be appropriate to facilitate change with a minimum of resistance? The
personnel manager should be able to offer advice, drawing upon his expertise in
the behaviourial sciences and the great deal of empirical research in this area.

When planning any change, but particularly those involving new technology, it is important to understand what Trist and Bamforth called the 'sociotechnical system'. In other words, it must be recognised that a technical process will determine work patterns which in turn create social groups. If these groups are disrupted due to technological change, the projected increases in output may not materialise due to resistance from the workforce.

It is generally agreed that when introducing change it is preferable to involve those who will be affected at the planning stage. Several researchers, including Coch and French, Likert and Lawler *et al*, have concluded that where a high degree of participation has accompanied change a minimum of disruption and loss of production has resulted. However, participation in change is not sufficient in itself and may be suspected in an organisation which has previously been managed autocratically. The change itself must also be perceived as legitimate by those affected. All implications of the change must be communicated at an early stage in order to allay fears already referred to and where a major change is planned it is advisable to consult worker representatives at all stages.

Where an organisation has particular problems of coping with change due to human relations difficulties, it might be advisable to consider organisation development (OD). This is a strategy employed by some organisations with a view to improving the ability of individuals and work groups to solve problems in a more open and constructive manner. It usually employs an external 'change agent' who diagnoses the situation and uses various techniques to encourage open discussion of problems and assist teams in working together towards mutually set objectives. Many claims of success have been made for OD programmes, particularly where there has been resistance and lack of communication at management levels. The strategy is not a 'cure-all', however, and may not be effective for all situations.

To summarise, there is clear evidence that change can precipitate strong resistance. If management is to avoid or at least minimise this resistance, it should attempt to build some of the above points into its management policies. If, however, these policies are not to appear hollow there will have to be a real and overall change in management philosophy from 'Theory X' to 'Theory Y' in McGregor's terms.

Further examination questions

1 Describe the major technological developments which are likely to affect banking in the foreseeable future. What changes are likely to result for customers, employees and management? (*IOB*)

2 What are the current economic, social and political trends which are likely to be of most importance for banking over the next decade? Explain their significance. (*IOB*)

3 A manager colleague has come to you for advice as to how to plan and implement a change in the staffing and working methods of his

department. What considerations would you suggest he takes into
account?   (*IPM*)

4 Examine in general terms (but with specific examples if possible) the
contribution which a personnel manager can make to the redesign
or restructuring of an organisation.   (*ICSA*)

5 It is often said that the status of the personnel function has
improved immeasurably in the last decade or so. What are the major
factors accounting for this change? In what ways do you consider
that the role and position of the personnel function are likely to alter
in the next ten years?   (*ICSA*)

6 Under what circumstances might it be advisable to use a 'third
party' change agent to assist the management of change? What kind
of third party could you bring in, how would you use that person(s)
and what problems might arise?   (*IPM*)

General comments on questions

Although all the above questions refer to change in general terms they vary considerably in emphasis and also in subject matter. Several of them are quite
speculative and certainly have no 'correct' answer. It is usually with these types
of question that the examiner is testing powers of reasoning and logical thought
rather than technical expertise. This in no way implies that the subject matter
can be absolute rubbish provided it is well put together! It is rather to point out
that questions in this area are more likely to be successfully attempted by the
well-read and thoughtful candidate than by those who prefer to 'learn' material
in a stereotyped way.

Questions 1 and 2, whilst demanding a degree of technical knowledge,
require that this knowledge is employed in developing a well-reasoned account
of the impact and significance of the developments referred to. Although they
both refer to banking, they could appear in the context of any business
enterprise.

Question 1 should not present much difficulty regarding technological
developments, as most candidates will be aware of the various applications of
micro-processor hardware. It is probably in the area of human impact that most
weakness would be exposed. Matters such as training and deployment of staff,
manpower planning, job satisfaction, redundancy, industrial relations, structure, communications spring to mind as worthy of mention in respect of both
management and staff. Customers will presumably look forward to a 'better',
albeit less personal, service.

Question 2 is in a very similar vein although the net is cast much wider than
mere technology. Again the examiner will be looking for a sound and well-
reasoned account of the types of development referred to. Their significance for
banking should then be discussed in terms of such matters as business development, investment, ownership, industrial relations, staffing etc.

Question 3 is to a large extent covered by the suggested answer to the sample examination question above. Good advice would presumably cover attention to such things as:
– Resistance to change.
– Organisational 'climate'.
– Attitudes.
– Work groups and group cohesiveness.
– Consultation and participation.
– Motivation for change.

This advice could be based upon the great deal of research and practical experience in the area of human relations and change.

Questions 4 and 5 both concern the role of the personnel manager, although the former is rather more specific in that it concentrates on a particular operation.

Question 4 requires an examination of the personnel manager's potential contribution to organisational redesign or restructure. It is assumed that the development in question will involve the staff of the organisation to a considerable degree and we are consequently in the areas of recruitment, redeployment, training, redundancy and so on. We also assume that the specific examples referred to would be in one or more of these activities. It should not be too difficult to refer to examples of, for instance, the ways in which redundancy and redeployment policies, properly discussed and drawn up in advance, would assist with a major restructuring (see Section 15 on redundancy). A more comprehensive answer might also include the matters discussed earlier in this section concerning the psychological and social problems associated with change and the industrial relations and other problems which may arise if it is not handled carefully. The personnel manager should certainly be able to bring his experience to bear in this context.

Question 5 provides an opportunity for a degree of speculation, although this will need to be based upon sound knowledge of the personnel profession. A logical approach might be to consider some of the main trends in areas such as social change, unionisation, organisational size and structure, legislation etc and extrapolate these into the future.

Question 6 is more specifically concerned with organisation development (OD) activities and should not be tackled by those without a sound knowledge of the subject. W. G. Bennis has acted as a 'change agent' on many occasions and has written a great deal about it. He is by profession a psychologist and although many consultants in this field have a similar background it is not essential for success in this role. Bennis states that 'Organisation development is necessary whenever our social institutions compete for survival under conditions of chronic change'. He then goes on to describe threats and pressures upon organisations such as rapid growth, change in managerial attitudes, demands for new skills and technological change. There are various objectives which are generally shared by most OD consultants concerned with creating a more open and trustful climate and improving the problem-solving skills of those within the organisation. Various techniques will be employed to achieve these goals but most of them are concerned with making the staff of the organisation more aware of their own attitudes and the way in which they relate to their colleagues. Meetings, discussion groups, questionnaires, interviews and training sessions form part of the armoury of techniques available.

OD is, like any other activity, not without its critics. Some consider it to be too ambitious, long-term and consequently expensive. It tends to concentrate on human relations problems at the expense of structural and technical problems and often fails to solve problems in the longer term. There are recognised prerequisites for even a fair chance of success and without these any programme is probably doomed to failure.

Although we have only scratched the surface in discussing points raised by this particular examination question, it is hoped that we have illustrated the danger of attempting questions of this type without adequate reading on the subject. Those who have not acquired the necessary degree of knowledge are referred to the recommended reading list below.

Recommended reading

Brooks, E., *Organisational Change: The Managerial Dilemma*, Macmillan, 1980.

Margerison, C., *Influencing Organisational Change*, IPM, 1978.

Bennis, W. G., *Organisation Development: Its Nature, Origins, and Prospects*, Addison-Wesley, 1969.

Bristow J., Carby, K. and Thakur, M., *Personnel in Change*, IPM, 1978.

Pratt, K. J. and Bennett, S. G., *Elements of Personnel Management*, Gee & Co. Ltd, 1979 (Chaps. 26–27)